Unlocking

Creativity

Teaching Across the Curriculum

Edited by
Robert Fisher • Mary Williams

David Fulton Publishers

Related titles of interest:

Unlocking Literacy   Fisher and Williams (1 85346 652 2)
Unlocking Writing   Williams (1 85346 850 9)
Unlocking Numeracy   Koshy and Murray (1 85346 835 5)

David Fulton Publishers
2 Park Square, Milton Park, Abingdon, Oxon OX14 4RN

270 Madison Avenue, New York, NY 10016

First published 2004 by David Fulton Publishers
Transferred to digital printing

David Fulton Publishers is an imprint of the Taylor & Francis Group, an informa business

Copyright © 2004 Robert Fisher, Mary Williams and the individual contributors

British Library Cataloguing in Publication Data
A catalogue record for this book is available from the British Library.

ISBN 1 84312 092 5

Typeset by RefineCatch Ltd, Bungay, Suffolk

Contents

Acknowledgements

We would like to thank the many teachers, students and children who have helped to inform our research into creativity. We have welcomed the collaboration with colleagues from different institutions, as well as with those from within our own department at Brunel. Every effort has been made to obtain permission to include copyright material in this book. In case of failure to obtain permission, the editors and publishers undertake to make good any omissions in future printings.

Notes on contributors

David Barlex is an acknowledged leader in the area of design & technology education, curriculum design and curriculum materials development. He is the Director of the Nuffield Design and Technology Projects, and through this activity has produced an extensive range of curriculum materials that are widely used in primary and secondary schools in England, Scotland and Wales. He is the educational manager of the Young Foresight Initiative and through this has developed an interest in developing approaches to teaching and learning that enable young people to respond creatively to design & technology activities.

Lynne Broadbent is Director of the British and Foreign Schools Society's National Religious Centre at Brunel University, and is currently managing a national project on religious education and school effectiveness. She is engaged in teacher education for primary and secondary students, in-service training and consultancy within LEAs, and is a Section 23 inspector. She has written on the contribution of RE within the school curriculum to Values and Citizenship Education and to pupils' spiritual, moral, social and cultural development. Her research interest is in the relationship between subject knowledge and pedagogy.

Juliet Edmonds is a senior lecturer in science education at the University of the West of England. Formerly, she worked at Brunel University for ten years and in west London schools as an advisory teacher for primary science and assessment. Her research interests lie in Assessment for Learning in science and science for children with English as an additional language.

Robert Fisher is Professor of Education and Director of the Centre for Research in Teaching Thinking at Brunel University. His research and publications on teaching thinking are internationally recognised and he has published more than 20 books on education. His recent publications include *Teaching Thinking* (Continuum) and the highly acclaimed *Stories for Thinking* series (Nash Pollock). He is involved in research and training with schools and local education authorities, is an adviser to the UK

Department for Education and Skills, and is a frequent speaker at national and international conferences on teaching literacy, creativity and thinking skills.

Andrew Green taught English in a variety of schools in Oxfordshire and London before becoming Head of English at Ewell Castle School, Surrey. He now lectures in Education at Brunel University, working on both undergraduate and post-graduate courses. He has contributed articles on many texts to *The English Review*. He is the author of a Philip Allan Teacher Resource Pack on Gothic literature and Student Text Guides on *Frankenstein, Wuthering Heights* and *Songs of Innocence and of Experience*.

Colleen Johnson spent several years as an actor in Canada and the UK, working mainly in theatre in education, co-founding two theatre companies. She has a wide range of teaching experience, specialising in drama, voice production and lecturing skills. She is a Senior Lecturer in Drama in Primary Education at St Mary's University College, Twickenham.

Valsa Koshy is Reader in Education at Brunel University. Prior to joining the University she was an advisory teacher for mathematics. She co-ordinates the mathematics in-service programme at the University and teaches mathematics to Initial Training students. She is also Director of the Brunel Able Children's Education (BACE) Centre. She has published a number of practical books on the teaching of mathematics.

Sara Liptai has experimented with secondary teaching, translated Hungarian poetry into English and worked in radio journalism. While primary teaching she became interested in Philosophy for Children. Since completing her PhD on using music in philosophical enquiry she has trained teachers for Philosophy for Children and collaborated in a number of philosophy projects including one aimed at using drama and philosophy to foster better understanding between Muslim and non-Muslim pupils.

Avril Loveless has written extensively on creativity and ICT in education. She is a member of Creating Spaces, a lobby group for creative use of new technologies in schools, in collaboration with the Arts Council of Great Britain, and is an editor of the journal *Technology, Pedagogy and Education*.

Fran Martin is Senior Lecturer in Primary Geographical Education at University College, Worcester. She is also a trustee for The World Studies Trust and does some in-service training for Worcester LEA and Birmingham Development Education Centre. Fran's interests are in creativity and thinking skills in primary geography, geographical learning in the Foundation Stage and the contribution of geography to children's development as global citizens.

Debbie Robinson has worked in education for over twenty years as a classroom teacher, advisory teacher and teacher trainer. Her work involved research on both the Graded Assessments in Mathematics and TVEI and Mathematics projects. She is currently employed as a Senior Lecturer at St Mary's University College, Twickenham, and as a mathematics consultant for Beam Education and for the Royal Borough of Kensington and Chelsea.

Rupert Wegerif has written and researched extensively on the role of new technology supporting learning dialogues in classrooms. He is based at the Open University where he leads the Educational Dialogue Research Unit. He writes a regular column for the magazine *Teaching Thinking*. More information and papers are available on his website: fels-staff.open.ac.uk/rupert-wegerif/

Mary Williams taught for 20 years as a primary school teacher, the last nine as head teacher of a nursery/infant school. She is a part-time Senior Research Fellow at Brunel University with research interests that include literacy learning, educating pupils in the early years and metacognition. She also works for the Brunel Able Children's centre and as a freelance education consultant. She is co-editor and editor respectively of *Unlocking Literacy* and *Unlocking Writing* and has published widely in language and literacy fields.

Introduction

'Creativity is about being able to do things and to live your life in a better way.'

(Jemma, aged 10)

CREATIVE THINKING SKILLS ARE ESSENTIAL for success in learning and success in life. They are key skills that underpin the National Curriculum in England and should be promoted across all subjects of the curriculum. There is potential for creative thinking in all fields of human activity, and in every lesson. This book offers a review of strategies for creative teaching and learning across the curriculum. It aims to identify ways to develop children's capacity for originality and creative achievement.

Promoting creative thinking is a powerful way of engaging children with their learning. Children who are encouraged to think creatively show increased levels of motivation and self-esteem. Creativity prepares them with the flexible skills they will need to face an uncertain future. Employers want people who are adaptable, innovative, can solve problems and communicate well with others. Developing the capacity to be creative can enrich lives and help to contribute to a better society.

Creativity is not just about the arts, or particular types of individual; we all have the capacity for creative thinking – for generating and extending ideas, suggesting hypotheses, applying imagination and looking for alternative innovative outcomes in any activity. Creativity means generating outcomes that are original and of value. Originality may be in relation to one's previous experience, or to that of a group, or it may be uniquely original in terms of what is already known and thought in the world. Creative thinking is also about judgement – the ability to judge the value of ideas and outputs.

Creative children need creative teachers, but there can be many blocks to creativity. One block to creativity may be defensive teaching. There is little chance for creativity where pupils work for long periods of time with low demand and little active input, where outcomes are controlled and prescribed, and where complex topics are taught in superficial ways. Creativity thrives where there is time to explore, experiment and play with ideas. Children need the right conditions for creativity to flourish.

Creative thinking is shown when children generate outcomes, show imagination and originality and can judge the value of what they have done. What promotes creativity is a questioning classroom, where teachers and pupils ask unusual and challenging questions; where new connections are made; where ideas are represented in different ways – visually, physically and verbally; where there are fresh approaches and solutions to problems; and where the effects of ideas and actions are critically evaluated.

We believe that all lessons can develop creative thinking when they involve pupils in generating and extending ideas, suggesting hypotheses, applying imagination and finding new or innovative outcomes. The contributors to this book aim to help you increase the opportunities for creativity in the lessons you teach. To check whether a lesson has stimulated creative thinking we need to look for evidence of pupils:

- applying their imagination;

- generating their own questions, hypotheses, ideas and outcomes;

- developing skills or techniques through creative activity; and

- using judgement to assess their own or others' creative work.

Creative children need creative teachers and it is no surprise that the most successful schools, as identified by Ofsted inspectors, place a strong emphasis on creativity in teaching and learning. But how do we find the time for creativity in an already overcrowded curriculum? One answer is to cut down on detailed coverage of the core curriculum and give more time to a creative curriculum devised by schools themselves.

China and other countries in the Far East are placing an emphasis on the creative curriculum because they know that future personal, social and economic success depends on creative thinking skills. We also have good reason to foster a creative curriculum in the UK; school inspectors have found that those schools with the most imaginative and creative approach to the curriculum – schools that interpret the curriculum within their own clear philosophy – tend to get both the best results and inspection reports (Ofsted 2002, cited in Chapter 1).

As teachers, we may not be in charge of the curriculum but we are in charge of our classrooms and schools. All that is needed is the confidence to adapt and innovate the basic curriculum (including literacy and numeracy hours), do extended projects, make links across the curriculum and build creative thinking skills into all aspects of teaching.

So how should we start? A Chinese proverb says that 'a journey of a thousand miles begins with one step'. Evidence suggests that thinking big, with a bold vision, but starting small, is the best recipe for success. The unit of change may be one lesson. We need the confidence to do more than the National Curriculum prescribes, more than what can simply be tested. Creative teaching requires one to take risks, including teaching that emphasises not just short-term objectives but the long-term benefits of a thinking and creative curriculum. Creativity is central to the curriculum, not a marginal 'extra'. It is a key to human flourishing in uncertain, problematic times.

This book aims to shows what creativity is and how it can be learned. Ways to foster creativity across the curriculum are presented, illustrated and discussed. The book will interest all involved in seeking to develop creative minds and to foster creative communities of learning with children from 4–14 years, at the Foundation Stage and in Key Stages 1, 2 and 3.

Creativity is an elusive and problematic concept. In Chapter 1 Robert Fisher asks the questions 'What is creativity?' and 'Why is it important?'. He sets out to define what creativity is and to show how it is best developed in individuals, in classrooms and in schools. The chapter provides a rationale for what is to follow in the rest of the book. Creative thinking is seen as essential for successful learning and for ultimate success in life. It identifies the characteristics of creative organisations, of the creative curriculum and of creative teachers. It argues that creative schools produce more creative learners by focusing on developing not only core skills and knowledge but creative skills and attitudes that underpin lifelong learning.

In Chapter 2 Mary Williams shows how playfulness is central to creativity and explores how young pupils in the Foundation Stage and Key Stage 1 can learn literacy through creative, constructive and problem-solving play. In recent years play has sometimes been derided as a means of learning, but it can offer a challenging and motivating context for creative learning. Adults need to know how to intervene in children's play to sustain their interest and to challenge them to think more deeply about what they are doing. The chapter shows how the use of high levels of questioning can provide a good stimulus for deep thinking and creative learning.

In Chapter 3 Andrew Green investigates creative writing with older pupils and explores ways to help them find their 'creative voice'. He focuses on the ways in which creative writing is perceived and identifies some of the myths that surround it. He discusses the notion of creativity within the context of writing and explores a range of examples of creativity in the classroom. He explores the connections between reading, writing and creativity, and offers practical suggestions as to how creative writing can be encouraged and enhanced. The key to creativity, he argues, is through careful and sensitive teaching of the creative processes of writing and taking risks with words.

In Chapter 4 Colleen Johnson discusses ways in which teachers can use drama to enhance creative thinking, both individually and collaboratively. She argues that critical reflection lies at the heart of creative drama teaching and draws on examples from primary classrooms to illustrate this. A case is made for an increased recognition of the status of drama in schools and in teacher training, through the contribution it can make to creative thinking by getting pupils to think from within. Strategies for the classroom are explored from process to performance to show the key role that drama can play in unlocking the creativity of pupils.

In Chapter 5 Debbie Robinson and Valsa Koshy explore creativity in mathematics. They see it as central to mathematics teaching and offer practical ways to encourage teachers to cultivate creativity in their teaching and their pupils' learning. This is dependent on careful planning, involving procedures, application and elegance. It is important to provide a context that builds on children's natural creativity rather than textbook examples that lead them to claim that mathematics is boring.

Similarly, in Chapter 6 Juliet Edmonds suggests that teachers should build on children's ideas in science rather than offer them textbook views of what scientific knowledge is. Textbook views, she argues, can only ever be provisional. Children should be encouraged to think creatively about scientific problems, to raise hypotheses and to plan and evaluate outcomes from as many perspectives as possible. They need to be helped to think carefully and creatively about the evidence collected, and to see if emerging patterns lead them to change or develop their initial ideas. She offers practical examples from the classroom to show how creative science teaching can be put into practice.

In Chapter 7 Avril Loveless and Rupert Wegerif investigate ways in which Information and Communications Technology (ICT) can help develop children's creativity. They stress that it is not just the characteristics of ICT, or particular software, that determine if an educational activity is creative but also how ICT is used by teachers and children to support creative learning. They offer practical examples across the curriculum to show how ICT can be used to stimulate the imagination of children, help them make meaning, share their work and evaluate outcomes. Teachers have a vital role in planning stimulating opportunities for creativity through ICT.

In Chapter 8 David Barlex discusses of the relationship between design & technology and creativity. Findings from a current QCA/Nuffield research project are presented which develop a model for creative teaching in the classroom. The creative work of children in Key Stage 2 and Key Stage 3 illustrates the author's view that without creativity the promise of design & technology will be reduced to the acquisition of technical skills without purpose. Through design & technology pupils can learn how to intervene creatively to improve their quality of life. Creative teaching can help pupils, as individuals and in teams, to become creative thinkers and problem solvers.

Chapter 9 shows how and why geography has potential as a subject to develop creative thinking in ways that are meaningful and relevant to children's lives. Fran Martin does so by examining the subject, the teacher and the learner. She argues that a key to creativity is the creation of 'possible worlds' and discusses ways to adapt the curriculum to be more creative. She uses illustrations from classroom work to explore implications for teachers' practice and children's learning. Reference is also made to historical enquiry to show how cross-curricular work can strengthen creative thinking and geographical learning.

In Chapter 10 Sara Liptai advocates an approach to the music and art & design curriculum based on an intellectually challenging group discussion format derived from *Philosophy for Children* called the 'community of enquiry'. This stems from the notion that children should be empowered to participate creatively and actively in their own education through thinking about problems or questions that have significance to them. A number of practical examples are offered to show how the 'collaborative conversation' that takes place in a community of enquiry can be a source of effective and sustained learning for children in the arts.

In Chapter 11 Lynne Broadbent explores the concept of creativity in relation to religion and its contribution to pupils' religious education and spiritual development. The chapter draws upon current theories and approaches to religious education and examines these with reference to classroom practice. It argues that religions, in essence, are dynamic and are about change and creativity. The danger is that of a fragmented curriculum full of unrelated content. Pupils need to be creatively engaged in reflection, empathetic imagination and interpretation of religious questions and experience. These skills can only be developed through a creative approach to teaching religious education.

In Chapter 12 Robert Fisher argues that creativity is important across the curriculum and presents teaching strategies to show how a creative approach to teaching can be applied to any lesson in any subject with any group of children. Creativity can be developed in any curriculum area, as examples in this book show, but it also needs promoting through a policy and vision which embrace the whole school. Case studies of two schools which emphasise creativity across the curriculum are presented and discussed. Finally, a number of review questions provide a stimulus for discussing ways of developing a policy for developing creativity across the curriculum.

In summary, creative pupils need creative teachers and teachers need to work in schools where creativity is valued and shared. Jemma, aged 10, when asked what creativity was suggested that 'creativity is about being able to do things and to live your life in a better way'. We need the courage to be creative in our teaching – and to put creativity at the heart of the curriculum. This book sets out to show how this can be achieved.

What is creativity?

Robert Fisher

'Imagination is more important than knowledge. For knowledge is limited while imagination embraces the whole world.'

(Albert Einstein)

'Creativity is not just art. It is thinking deeply and having original thoughts about something.'
(Georgie Eccles, aged 10, from Westbury Park School, Bristol)

IN A RECENT COMPETITION teachers were asked to set their own 'targets for creativity' for the children in their schools.[1] The entries had much in common. They nearly all wanted to ensure children had a wide range of experience, not only for intellectual but also for personal and cultural development. Among the more unorthodox creativity targets included were:

- dance until your legs ached
- play in the snow
- care for an animal
- admire a rainbow.

But in what ways are these objectives creative? What makes an experience, thought or activity creative? This chapter seeks answers to the questions: What is 'creativity'? Why is it important? How is it best developed in individuals, in classrooms and in schools?

In the Victorian era there was little room for creativity in British schools. It was a time of 'payment by results' and of rote learning. The common idea of education in those days was that of memorisation; and a regime of central control, inspection and testing ensured little time for creativity. In recent years, for many teachers in England, this has sounded like a familiar regime.

Although interest in creativity goes back to the ancient world, what is now thought of as the 'creativity movement' began in Europe and America after the Second World War. There were two impulses for this. First, there was the perceived need to train scientists, engineers and designers to be more creative and innovative in response to global competition. Second, there was a reaction against prevailing values that were seen as excessively bureaucratic and manipulative. In the classroom this meant wanting to shake education free from excessive testing and rote learning and to encourage more open-ended, student-centred learning. There was a new focus on the arts and creativity to broaden the basic curriculum. A pamphlet of advice to teachers, published in the 1940s and '50s spoke of 'unlocking the minds and opening the shut chambers of the hearts' of the deprived postwar generation.[2] There followed much research into the nature of creativity and innovation, into the lives of creative people and the processes of creative thinking.

The postwar flowering of the arts and creativity had many benefits, but it had a downside in that many teachers forgot about the importance of the 'basics'. Hence, in England, as elsewhere, came the backlash of the 'back to basics' movement that resulted in a more prescribed curriculum. In recent years there has been a renewed interest in creativity – not just in the arts but also across the curriculum – fostered in England by the publication of Ken Robinson's seminal report in 1999.[3] Since then a new consensus has grown around the view that attending to the basics and encouraging creativity, far from being mutually exclusive, are both needed for success in learning and in life. However, the question remains: What is creativity?

What is creativity?

The trouble with creativity, as with intelligence and other brain-based functions, is that the concept is ethereal and elusive. Years of research has gone into trying to specify what creativity is, but despite all the checklists, models and tests, researchers admit that we do not know how fully to explain the creative power of the brain. We lack a proper language to describe the brain activity associated with creativity. We know creativity when we see it but the mental processes involved are difficult to describe. As a student once said to me, 'If I knew what creativity meant I'd know if I was creative'. What follows is an attempt to describe what creativity is and how it can be fostered.

If we ask, 'What is creativity?' we are asking, in a Socratic sense, what all examples of creativity have in common by virtue of which they are creative. More exactly, we are looking for the necessary and sufficient conditions for creativity. The assumption here is that creativity is a type of thing – something with an essence or nature. Creativity may not have an exact nature. We can say with precision what all triangles have in common, by virtue of which they are triangles, but the concept of creativity seems to be fuzzy at the edges. However, a good definition of creativity will help us to identify what it is we are talking about, why certain things are clearly creative and others are not.

Many attempts have been made to define creativity. Howard Gardner (1997) has described it as 'the ability to solve problems and fashion products and to raise new questions'. Bill Lucas (2001) says that it is 'a state of mind in which all our intelligences are working together', and Ken Robinson (2001) states that it is 'imaginative processes with outcomes that are original and of value'. Part of the reason for this diversity of definitions is that creativity can be seen as a property of people (who we are), processes (what we do) or products (what we make). I will argue that the processes that underpin creativity also underpin the evolution of life.

Processes of creative evolution

The principle processes of creative evolution are:

- generation
- variation
- originality.

To create is to generate something. At the simplest level creativity is making, forming or bringing something into being. To create is to be productive in thought, word or deed. The first principle of evolution, of creative minds and schools, is that of generation. In the natural world organisms must produce more progeny than are needed. The same principle applies to ideas. Generating outputs such as ideas, experiments and innovations is a necessary part of creative effort. When Linus Pauling, the Nobel Prize-winning chemist, was asked how he had come up with so many creative discoveries he replied: 'It's easy; you think of a lot of ideas, and throw away the bad ones'. Creativity begins with generation or bringing forth – whether it be ideas, designs or species. However, generation by itself is not sufficient for creativity. Bees make honey and ants make nests through instinctive activity. Machines make cars through mechanical activity. Much that we do may be the result of routine and habit. We should not confuse mere generative activity with creativity.

Every organism or member of a species (including teachers) varies in some way from every other one. The second principle of creativity is differentiation. To be creative outputs must be varied. Creativity is not evidenced in mere repetition. Andy Warhol, the artist, generated images of multiple copies of Campbell's soup cans in his art, but each work contained images that were variations on the original design – hence they were creative. Creative teachers do not merely repeat lessons, they add to them and vary them. New knowledge and better adaptation derives from exploratory processes that seek to vary what is given. The most effective primary schools are characterised by innovation in teaching and an emphasis on developing pupils' creativity and self-confidence according to an Ofsted report on successful primary schools.[4] Variation is the exploratory process of evolution. We need to adapt to survive. Those who do not adapt become like the dinosaurs – extinct. Creativity, like evolution and education, is founded on experimentation, variations that sometimes succeed, sometimes fail. Creativity, therefore, requires the courage to take risks – the risk to be different.

Where evolution succeeds in creative adaptation aspects of these variations are inherited by offspring. Unique features, when effective, are adopted and further adapted by others. Jerome Bruner (1962) defines creativity as 'an act that produces *effective surprise'*. It is originality that provides effective surprise. To do the same things in the same way is not to be creative, to do things differently adds variation to mere habit, but when we do or think things we have not done or thought before, and they are effective, we are being original and fully creative. Such originality is a matter of degree. Some things may be original to an individual mind, some original within a group or community and some are universally unique.

Degrees of originality

- individual: being original in relation to one's previous thoughts, words or deeds, e.g. 'I have not thought or done this before';

- social: being original in relation to one's social group, community or organisation, e.g. 'We have not thought or done this before';

- universal: being original in terms of all previous known human experience, e.g. 'No-one has thought or done this before'.

A creative act is of value if it generates something novel, original or unique. Creativity is important and of educative value because, in whatever field it occurs, it adds something new to human knowledge and/or experience, although that something new may not at the time be recognised as 'valuable' or 'useful' by others. The history of art and science is littered with examples of original ideas that were at first, or for a long time, rejected. We would not want to say that Stravinsky's *Rite of Spring*, or Copernican theory was not creative because it was rejected by many experts at the time. A creative act or idea may or may not be given the seal of approval by others. Being creative may mean going beyond the limits (or targets or curriculum) set by others. For schools it may mean creating their own recipes for excellence, rather than following the recipes of others.

Creativity can be thought of as embodied imagination. Imaginative activity is the process by which we generate something that is original. As Miercoles, aged 10, from Westbury Park School put it, 'Creativity is like imagination because when you create something you need to imagine it first'. What imagination does is to enable the mind to represent images and ideas of what is not actually present to the senses. It can refer to the capacity to predict, plan and foresee possible future consequences. In short, imagination is the capacity to conceive possible (or impossible) worlds that lie beyond this time and place. These possible worlds may derive from actual worlds reproduced from our store of memories. As William Blake said: 'What is now proved was once imagined'.

Imagination is both reproductive and productive. 'Reproductive imagination' is the capacity to represent in the mind external objects that are absent as if they were present, as when we bring to mind remembered experiences, as in: 'I can imagine being there now' or 'It happened like this'. Reproductive imagination is characteristic of adaptors – people who build on or adapt existing ideas. 'Productive imagination' is the mind's ability to form concepts beyond those derived from external objects. Productive imagination is characteristic of innovators who fuse new concepts out of existing ideas.

'Imagination rules the world,' said Napoleon. It is the faculty that provides colour to our lives and underpins our curiosity and wonder. It is essential not only to creativity but also to our capacity to respond to and appreciate the creativity of others. It informs our emotional lives, including our ability to understand ourselves and others. The downside of imagination is that it feeds fantasy and false belief. Plato banished artists from his ideal Republic on the grounds that imagination distorts reality, creates illusions and encourages people to feel rather than think. Imagination can be used to serve evil ends, so it needs to be informed by values; it can lead to false belief, so it needs to be tempered by critical thinking, reasoning and judgement.

Many writers differentiate these two kinds of thinking – the creative and the critical – using a range of terms to describe these processes, including:

Creative thinking	Critical thinking
synthesis	analysis
divergent	convergent
lateral	vertical
possibility	probability
imagination	judgement
hypothesis forming	hypothesis testing
subjective	objective
an answer	the answer
right brain	left brain
open-ended	closed
associative	linear
speculating	reasoning
intuitive	logical
yes and	yes but

We need both critical and creative thinking, both analysis and synthesis, both the parts and the whole to be effective in our thinking. We need both reason and intuition, order and adventure in our thinking. We need creative thinking to generate the new, but critical thinking to make judgements about it. The technological world gives us access to knowledge in abundance, but creativity is in short supply.

Why is creativity important?

What is, is, but it doesn't have to be or stay this way. The message of creativity is: you can do something with what you are given, to change it. The world, as it is presented to us, is not the only possible world. Through our imagination we can use it as a model for other possible worlds. Aspects of the world may be inadequate to our vision of what might be or should be. We may want to lift the world beyond some of the routine, mediocre and sterile visions of the present. The artist Paul Klee expressed this ambitious purpose when he said: 'I do not wish to portray man as he is but only as he might be'. Creative minds exercise freedom of thought, they are able to think beyond the given, beyond the world of necessity, and to engage in thought-experiments, thereby to imaginatively create possible worlds out of the raw materials of this world. Such creative impulses are not just idle fancies; they are vital factors in personal, social, economic and educational success.

The challenge for schools and social institutions is clear: the focus of education must be on creating people who are capable of thinking and doing new things, not simply repeating what past generations have done, but equipped for a world of challenge and change. Creativity is essential if new ways are to be found of solving problems. Creativity is also rewarding at an emotional level. It offers individuals the spontaneous pleasures of play, self-expression and satisfaction. During creative activity, freed from the burden of necessity, many people experience their greatest joy – what Csikszentmihalyi (1992) calls 'flow'. Creative activity in any sphere offers challenge, what Yeats called 'the fascination of what's difficult'. At an educational level creativity enhances academic performance. Research by Robert Sternberg (1999) shows that when students are assessed in ways that recognise and value their creative abilities, their academic performance improves. Creative activity can rekindle the interest of students who have been turned off by school, and teachers who may be turned off by teaching in a culture of control and compliance.

Our society was built and developed by practical people who used their imaginations to build on the ideas of earlier generations, but some of our socially constructed world, including the world of educational policy, is the result of sterile vision, inadequate imagination and disjointed ideas. Creativity is central to improving the functioning and development of society and of schools. Creativity is developed through intellectual engagement, purpose, energy and interactive tension with others. These positive, creative attributes are essential to citizens living in an increasingly complex, changing and challenging social environment and essential for teachers in schools. Creativity is also needed to manage conflicts of interest and argument. It requires imagination to understand others, and creativity to resolve conflict.

We live in a world where success is closely related to the creative application of good ideas. The traditional means of economic production were raw material, hard labour and money, but no longer. What organisations need, now more than ever, is the application of creativity to knowledge. To succeed we need not only to produce outcomes but to manage change – and those creative intangibles that add value to what we do. This is true of educational as well as commercial and domestic settings. The hard stuff of facts and materials needs the soft stuff of human creativity, of creative thinking and creative human relationships. Success lies in what we do with what we are given – the way that creative minds mould matter. We have good reason, therefore, to invest in creative capacity at individual, social and national levels.

Creativity

Creativity is a characteristic of:

- people – our self-esteem and confidence as creative people – who we are;
- processes – the creative skills and knowledge we can use – how we do things;
- products – the outcomes of our creative efforts – what we do.

Creativity in schools is about people. Alice, aged 10, from Westbury Park School, finds the chance to be creative 'really amazing because you get to put your own ideas in it'. It gives you the chance to express who you are, what you think and can do. Creativity is of value, as another child explains, because 'creativity comes from me'. Creative experience provides satisfaction and self-expression. Creativity builds what the researcher Bandura calls 'self-efficacy', that combination of self-esteem, awareness and competence that is the best predictor of success in life. Creativity also depends on standards of excellence. Skills and knowledge are needed to make outcomes that are worthwhile. The exercise of reflection and judgement are also needed to assess the value of creative effort. As one child put it: 'Everything that is created gives you something to think about'.

What teacher do you best remember from your school days? Was it the one who followed the curriculum and lesson objectives most closely, that was most punctual in marking books? Or was it the someone that fired your imagination and sparked in you a creative passion for some form of learning? Research with a wide range of people shows that it is more likely to be the latter. What we need is teaching not trapped in defensive or routine thinking, but teaching that is innovative. We need our children to experience the unpredictable, to experience paradox and uncertainty. They need lessons that produce effective surprise. They need also to reflect the processes of creativity – to plan, do and review their learning activities. Effective learners need creative teachers who provide both order and adventure, who are willing to do the unexpected and take risks. Effective teachers need creative school leaders.

Creative people work hard and continually improve ideas and solutions, by making gradual alterations and refinements to their works. Contrary to the mythology surrounding creativity, very, very few works of creative excellence are produced with a single stroke of brilliance or in a frenzy of rapid activity. Here is Beethoven describing his way of working:

> I carry my thoughts with me for a long time, often for a very long time before writing them down . . . I change many things, discard others and try again until I am satisfied; then, in my head, I begin to elaborate the work . . . the underlying idea never deserts me. It rises, it grows. I hear and see the image in front of me from every angle.

Newton claimed that what enabled him to make discoveries in mathematics and science was his ability to concentrate intently on a problem for hours, days and weeks on end. He also said that he stood on the shoulders of giants – others who had gone before and helped him to see further. Research shows that experts in any creative field take about ten years of practice before they produce a masterwork. Creative excellence in any field requires long-term interest and investment of effort, and this is also true of creative schools.

Creative people

The following are some characteristics of creative people:

- they are flexible;
- they connect ideas;
- they are unorthodox;
- they show aesthetic taste
- they are curious and inquisitive;
- they see similarities and differences; and
- they question accepted ways of doing things.

The trouble with creative people, whether they be teachers, pupils or plumbers, is that they often find it difficult to explain their creativity. Many creative breakthroughs occur through creative insight, when a problem is intuitively seen in a new way or from a fresh viewpoint. 'Logic is the instrument of certainty,' said the French scientist Poincaré, 'intuition is the instrument of discovery.' Creative people find it hard to say where creative insight comes from. When asked where his music came from the composer Elgar replied 'Out of the air'. Mozart said of his musical ideas: 'Whence and how they come I know not; nor can I force them'. What many creative people seem to need is a period of gestation to allow what researcher Guy Claxton calls 'soft thinking' to take place.

Bartlett (1959) described creativity as 'adventurous thinking', which he characterised as 'getting away from the main track, breaking out of the mould, being open to experience, and permitting one thing to lead to another'. Human beings are forever caught, the French poet Apollinaire (creator of calligrams) once said, between order and adventure, between the known path and the path less travelled. A creative approach means generating ideas, seeking variation and being prepared to make the more adventurous choice. So how do we foster adventurous, open-ended creative thinking in schools?

How do we foster creativity?

Creativity has its roots in everyday activities. The processes of creativity are not solely expressed through the arts. When we edit a sentence to make it sound more interesting, posit a hypothesis or add something new to a recipe we are being creative. Without small acts of creativity great acts of creativity would not be possible. When we take up a pencil to draw a sketch we are emulating, in a small way, what Picasso, Titian and other artists achieve. When we hum our own tune we are in the creative foothills of musical composition. When we think of a hypothesis to explain a natural phenomenon we emulate the creativity of scientists. Great acts of creativity have their genesis in the experience of children who move to music, find shapes pleasing or speculate on the way the world works.

Good schools foster natural impulses to creativity by building creative capital. Creative capital is difficult to define and measure. It is made up of what enables people to focus creatively on the task in hand and supports them in that task.

Creative capital

Creative capital is the sum of resources needed to tackle a task, including:

- the creative self – the skills, commitment and talent brought to the task;
- the creative environment – the creative resources needed; and
- the creative partnerships – learning partners that support one another.

Focusing on the creative task is necessary. Any individual, company or school that tries to tackle everything everywhere at once often, as a result, does nothing well, its energies sapped by overload. Diffusion of focus means a diffusion of energy. Research shows that creative people exercise their creativity in particular spheres. The creative person is focused. In an age of multiplying activities, the creative person stops believing they can master all things and every situation. There is no way we can attend to everything with the same creativity, energy and enthusiasm. Creative people and creative head teachers focus on those areas in which they can make a difference.

Certain key features seem to be common to all fields of creative endeavour. These help to build creative capacity in individual learners and in ourselves, for as Gandhi said: 'We must be the change we want to see in the world'.

Some of the keys to individual creativity are:

- motivation
- inspiration
- gestation
- collaboration.

The key to creativity is *motivation* – not having to but wanting to, and having a purpose to do so. Motivation is what we need to add value to creative effort. 'Passion' is a word often used to describe the way creative scientists and artists feel about their work. We need to know that what we do is worthwhile. Individual creativity needs to be fed by internal and external encouragement. Creativity needs the encouragement of others: encouraging of adults in the classroom, at home, in the workplace and in all positions of social leadership.

Another key to creativity is *inspiration*. It means being inspired by oneself or by others. Creativity thrives on curiosity, fresh input and rich domains of knowledge. According to Csikszentmihalyi (1996), 'the first step towards a more creative life is the cultivation of curiosity, that is the allocation of attention to things for their own sake'. It is possible to stimulate curiosity by being more observant and asking more questions. Curiosity is contagious, and there is no more important job a teacher, parent or friend can do than to instil a sense of wonder about the world and human experience. A creative climate must be created where models of creativity are shared and celebrated. 'Those who have changed the universe have never done it by changing officials,' said Napoleon, 'but always by inspiring the people.'

Curiosity thrives on fresh input both within the setting, be it classroom or workplace and beyond the setting. That fresh input might be a museum, meeting someone new, seeing a play, reading something that you don't usually have time to read, or doing something you have never done before. The best kind of inspiration comes from involvement. We must involve people in creative activities. Creative people look on life as a series of creative projects. They seek out whatever inspires them – or they seek to inspire others by exposing them to the most creative experiences they can find. They seek the best in the field relevant to their interests. They are not content with the second-rate. Inspiration from others provides the necessary spur to our own thinking and creative effort. We therefore need to find the people and create the environments that inspire us.

A third key to creativity is *gestation*, that is allowing time for creative ideas to emerge. Insight and intuition are often associated with creativity and these take time to emerge. Creative insight often results from processes that are unconscious and lie below the level of awareness. Modern western culture celebrates the quick fix, the sound-bite, the fleeting image, and neglects what Guy Claxton (1999) calls the 'undermind', the capacity we all have for quiet contemplation and time being set aside for long-term thinking and unconscious working-through of ideas. We need time to think things through at conscious and unconscious levels. In schools, both pupils and teachers need to be engaged in rich tasks in environments that value thinking and learning, not just teaching and testing.

A fourth key to creativity is *collaboration*, through the support of learning partners or a community. We are more creative when we have others to support us. In adults, creativity has too often been suppressed through education, but it is still there and can be reawakened. Often, all that's needed to be creative is to have a commitment to creativity and to take the time for it. When I asked a child to define creativity he said: 'It is something you are free to do in your own way'. When I asked him why this was important, he looked puzzled for a moment, then said: 'It is what we are here for'. But creative success depends on having a fertile ground where new ideas and activities can take root, an environment in which ideas can be created, tossed around, shared and tried out. For this you need creative partners who you know can multiply what you know and can do. It is others who can help you realise what Vygotsky called your 'zone of potential development', that halo of potential we all carry around with us that we could realise if only we had that 'significant others' – learning partners who help you be who you might become. They raise your capability. They enable you to reach out further than you might. Creative partnerships add to your creative power.

Creative partnerships

Creativity is enhanced through creative partnerships:

- creative pupils need creative teachers;
- creative teachers need professional learning conversations with colleagues;
- creative schools need to maximise creative partnerships in the community.

Creative schools develop creative partnerships both within and beyond their schools. Such creative partnerships not only include inviting others, like artists, poets and actors into school – but also scientists, designers and engineers.[5]

The creative school: building communities of creativity

We live in a world whose institutions are increasingly dominated by 'competence control'. We are frequently judged by external standards and performance indicators. In such a world it becomes increasingly difficult for individuals to show creativity and to achieve ends beyond the 'competent'. But moving beyond 'competence', beyond the routine, beyond the everyday, is essential if we are to move beyond where we are, and if we are to fulfil the potential of individuals and organisations. Competence in performance, and all that assists it – from information technology to setting targets to flushing toilets – is essential. But technology, competence and hygiene will only get you so far. They are necessary but not sufficient for a life fully lived. Creativity needs to be added to competence and the clue to how communities become more creative lies in the workings of the human brain.

The critical means of production in any school is small and grey and weighs a little over one kilogram. It is the human brain. Creativity is built into the way the brain works. The human brain is a gloriously complex and intricate whole; its interconnectivity allows similar cognitive functions to take place in different areas of the cortex. It is interconnectivity in nature that allows evolution, variation and differentiation to take place. We build communities of creativity by building inter-connectivity, networks of communication – the 'info-structure'. Your 'info-structure' in school is the way that others inform you, give you feedback and stimulate your activity, as well as the way you do it for yourself. What is true of your brain is true of any organisation that seeks to be intelligent or creative. Info-structure is more important than infrastructure – the physical organisation, the given components of the system (brain or other organisation). It is not what you have but what you do with it that is important. And part of what is important about what you do is how you connect with others and use the information they have to help you. The psychologist Carl Jung once said 'I need we to be fully I'. Success in any grand project needs help from others, means making alliances, means benefiting from the distributed intelligence of others – developing the 'info-structure' – interconnectivity through learning conversations with others.

To help children develop their ideas in creative ways requires a willingness to observe, listen and work closely with them. Focused engagement with pupils is achieved through dialogue, either in a one-to-one or group situation – a common feature of all good teaching. We need to be attentive in case we miss the 'creative moment' where a student needs help to move forward or to develop a creative idea. Creative dialogue is not always easy to sustain and develop; it requires the particular skills of listening, interpreting and evaluating; a good level of subject knowledge; and time. It also needs an environment in which creativity is recognised and celebrated. One approach to developing creative conversations is the 'community of enquiry' which facilitates the raising of questions and serious, sustained discussion of issues in hand, where individuals build on each others' ideas, and difference of opinion is valued.[6]

Research shows that organisations create conditions that either foster or inhibit creativity. Creativity cannot be left to chance, otherwise it withers on the vine or remains the private concern of individuals. It is easy in any organisation for creative individuals to become isolated. Indeed, many highly creative people tend to be self-focused, driven by internal goals, and this can be at odds with team-orientated activity needed in organisational settings. Although innovation stems from individual talent and creativity, it is the organisational context that enhances and channels creative potential into creative production. The characteristics of creative organisations mirror those of creative individuals; they also model the micro-creative processes of the brain and mirror the macro-processes of evolution.

Features of a creative school

The creative school is a place where individuals, pupils and teachers are:

- motivated
  - purpose, ultimate goals and shared destiny;
  - openness to new ideas, innovation and enquiry;
  - passion to succeed, willing to take risks, accepting difference and diversity;
- given time and responsibility for creative activity, involving:
  - all in the search for creative solutions;
  - being tolerant of mistakes in the search for better solutions;
  - avoiding impulsivity, allowing time for practice and for ideas to come;

- able to collaborate with partners to share creativity and ideas including:
  - learning partners to generate, extend and provide feedback on ideas;
  - collaborating as part of a team on creative projects and productions;
  - developing creative connections and links beyond the organisation.

Creativity also needs space. An example of the way one school has used its environment to motivate, give time and provide children with opportunities for creativ collaboration is Caol Primary School, situated in a council estate in the West Highlands. They had an unused room (Room 13) which ten years ago they turned into an art room run by the children, for use at any time of the day. Inspired by an artist-in-residence it has produced innovative, exciting and award-winning artwork.[7] Attendance and attainment at school has gone up, and they recently won an award for school improvement. The head believes that as a result of having been part of Room 13 the children will leave it as very different people.

In organisations, as in individuals, there are obstacles as well as spurs to creativity. In schools the main obstacle to creativity is a too heavily prescribed curriculum. Ideally, schools need to have something like a 50 per cent core curriculum for the generation of basic skills and subject knowledge and 50 per cent creative curriculum which allows teachers the freedom to create varied, diverse and creative learning opportunities for students. Some of the characteristics of a creative curriculum would include:

- projects or sustained themes as the basic collaborative model around which creative learning and skills are developed, focused on an overall goal or outcome and extended over time;

- portfolios (or CD-ROM) for every child as a record of achievement in learning and creativity including both self-evaluation and collaborative assessment; and

- productions as tangible creative outcomes shared through display, and publication within and beyond the educational setting.

Another obstacle to creativity is feeling over-stressed. People need the stimulus of challenge, but there is a wealth of evidence to suggest that when people feel threatened, pressurised, judged or stressed, they tend to revert to ways of thinking that are more conventional and less creative. The enemy of creativity is overload, innovation fatigue and the pressure of too many external demands. Creativity requires time and space for attentive engagement with worthwhile tasks. Creativity is inspired by example. Creative children need creative teachers. Creative teachers flourish in environments that value time given to individual and collaborative creativity. Teachers provide creative inspiration for their students where school leaders give them the freedom and permission to express their creativity.

The style in which creative teamwork is undertaken is critical to its success. Creative leadership is about enabling others to engage in creative discussion and make creative decisions. The role of the team leader is crucial in providing inspiration, access to time and resources and a safe environment in which experiment and contention can take place.

Teams have most creative potential when they reflect intellectual diversity. The best creative groups engage in collaborative conversations in which all can have their say, and in which all is open to question. Free-thinking, freedom from censure and creative tension are some of the characteristics of such groups. Left to their own devices organisations tend to split into divisions or groups who do not share information or insights. It is essential for innovation that communities of enquiry, workshops or think-tanks be created to bring together diverse elements to focus on specific challenges, questions or goals.

Creative schools produce more creative learners by focusing on developing not only core skills and knowledge but also those creative skills and attitudes that underpin lifelong learning. They provide the stimulus of fresh input. Creative teams need new recruits and new challenges. There must be interconnectivity within and beyond the group, like those creative schools that make both local creative partnerships and global links. Schools which promote creativity tend to be outward-looking, with links to schools in other countries and involvement in national competitions and arts events.

Creativity happens when you move out of the comfort zone, when you are challenged and when you are in contention with yourself or with others. Creativity happens when we have the confidence to make mistakes; it happens when we are not tied to narrow targets but allow the spirit of play and imagination to inform what we do. It means being open to chance and opportunity, to try the path less travelled, to be open to doubts and uncertainties in seeking to generate what is new and original. Characterising this approach is the primary teacher who tells her class: 'Expect the unexpected in my lesson'.[8] The unexpected occurs where teaching and learning are creative. Creativity happens in schools that foster imaginative activity that generates outcomes that are original and of value. Kerry, aged 10, expressed it this way: 'Creativity is when you are surprised by what you do – and it works!'

Notes

1   See *Times Educational Supplement*, 4 July 2003, p.16.

2   'Story of a school', an account of a tough inner-city school led by inspirational head Peter Stone was published by the Ministry of Education after the war and subsequently reprinted in the 1950s.

3   NACCCE (1999) *All Our Futures: Creativity, Culture and Education*. National Advisory Committee on Creative and Cultural Education Report. London: DfEE. The NACCCE report (p. 29) defined creativity as: 'Imaginative activity fashioned so as to produce outcomes that are both original and of value'.

4   Ofsted (2002) *The Curriculum in Successful Primary Schools*. London: Ofsted.

5   For information on Creative Partnership initiatives see www.creative-partnerships.com

6   For more on how to develop a Community of Enquiry in the classroom see Robert Fisher's *Teaching Thinking* and *Stories for Thinking* series.

7   Some of this creative work went on show at Tate Modern, and on websites www.art-works.org.uk and http://www.room13scotland.com/)

8   Quoted in the Ofsted report *Expecting the Unexpected: Developing Creativity in Primary and Secondary Schools* (2003).

Further reading

Bartlett, F. (1959) *Thinking*. New York: Basic Books.

Bruner (1962), cited by Nickerson in Sternberg (1999).

Claxton, G. (1999) *Wise Up: The Challenge of Lifelong Learning*. London: Bloomsbury.

Craft, A. (2000) *Creativity Across the Primary Curriculum*. London: Routledge.

Cropley, A. J. (2001) *Creativity in Education and Learning: A Guide For Teachers and Educators*. London: Kogan Page.

Csikszentmihalyi, M. (1992) *Flow: The Psychology of Human Happiness*. London: Rider.

Csikszentmihalyi, M. (1996) *Creativity*. New York: HarperCollins.

Design Council (2001) *Changing Behaviours*. London: Design Council/Campaign for Learning.

Fisher R. (1995) *Teaching Children to Think*. Cheltenham: Nelson Thornes.

Fisher, R. (1995) *Teaching Children to Learn*. Cheltenham: Nelson Thornes.

Fisher R. (1996) *Stories for Thinking*. Oxford: Nash Pollock.

Fisher R. (1997) *Games for Thinking*. Oxford: Nash Pollock.

Fisher R. (1998) *Teaching Thinking: Philosophical Enquiry in the Classroom*. London: Cassell.

Fisher R. (1999) *Head Start: How to Develop Your Child's Mind*. London: Souvenir Press.

Fisher R. (2001) *Values for Thinking*. Oxford: Nash Pollock.

Gardner, H. (1993) *Creating Minds*. New York: Basic Books.

Gardner, H. (1997) *Extraordinary Minds*. New York: HarperCollins.

Heppell, S. (1999) *Computers, Creativity, Curriculum and Children*. Cambridge: Anglia Polytechnic University Ultralab Website.

IDES (2001) *Creativity in Education*. Dundee: Learning and Teaching Scotland/IDES.

Lucas, B (2001) 'Creative teaching, teaching creativity and creative learning', in Craft, A., Jeffrey, B. and Leibling, M. (eds) *Creativity in Education*. London: Continuum.

NAACE (1999) *All Our Futures: Creativity, Culture and Education*. National Advisory Committee on Creative and Cultural Education Report. London: DfEE.

Robinson, K. (2001) *Out of Our Minds: Learning to Be Creative*. Oxford: Capstone.

Sternberg, R.J. (ed.) (1999) *Handbook of Creativity*. Cambridge: Cambridge University Press.

2

Creative literacy: learning in the early years

Mary Williams

'Auntie Betty's got two,' said Mark. 'Two what?' asked his puzzled mother. 'You know Bet . . . ty,' he replied, as he clapped the two syllables in her name. This incident happened when he was only three years old. He had learned about segmenting words through the clapping games he had played with his mother ever since he was a baby and was applying this knowledge creatively.

THIS CHAPTER LOOKS AT creative ways children learn literacy in the early years of education (three to seven years old). The relationship between play and learning is important because play encourages young children to think creatively while trying to solve problems that are very real to them at the time. The focus should be on learning through fun and enjoyment, as in the example above. It aims to show that play has potential in providing opportunities for creative thinking and learning.

Play

Play is a difficult concept to define but is taken here to mean all activities not imposed on children by adults.[1] It has a range of meanings and purposes. It can be free-flowing activity that captures the imagination. Sometimes, in relation to literacy, it can arise through hearing stories or poems read aloud. This encourages imaginative play that is often ludic in quality, for example when using the imagination during fantasy play by starting with the words 'Let's pretend . . .'.[2] Children often plan in elaborate detail during such play when discussing, for example, what they will do if they are going to pretend to travel through space. A conversation may go like this:

> Let's pretend we are going up in a spaceship. You can be the commander and I will be the one who closes the hatch door that came open after we took off. We can travel to the Moon and land there. We can meet the Man in the Moon and ask him what he has to eat, what he does in his spare time and whether he has any friends. Darren, you can be the Man in the Moon, if you like . . .

Play can be structured so that it forms part of a process of acculturation through which children learn about the social and physical world into which they have been born, for example by playing 'mothers and fathers' or 'schools' or 'hospitals'. It can include games and activities, self-initiated and pursued for purposes of amusement. For example, Kay, who at five years old already knows that she wants to be a teacher when she grows up, sets out her dolls in rows like in her class at school and writes worksheets for them to do, thus acting out a common role found in society. Play can be enhanced when adults take part in it to give it a focus and shape. For example, an adult could take on the role of a bus driver, after a line of chairs has been formed to be a bus, with the children, as passengers, being taken to visit different shops or locations and being asked to imagine and discuss what they might find there.

Play has long been recognised as an effective means of learning. Plato was one of the first to realise this, and down through the ages influential voices have built on his ideas.[3] Play is creative in that it provides *intrinsic motivation* through *self-initiated activities*. These, in turn, *foster children's imaginations* as imaginary worlds and scenarios are created as they *interact with the environment* in which they live. It enables them to experiment freely and to hypothesise about the world around them. Play is therefore very important for human development, and nowhere is this more important than in the learning of literacy.[4] However, if it is to serve educational purposes it needs to be purposeful, as already indicated, and requires the intervention of supportive adults, who help children think about what they are doing and provide them with opportunities to explore, experiment and play with ideas. Above all, teachers need to create an environment that stimulates creativity through, for example:

- leaving something unusual or out of place in a specific area of the classroom;

- putting written messages on displays or notices to incite curiosity;

- doing, or wearing, something out of character to inspire children to ask 'Why?';

- bringing unfamiliar artefacts or photographs into the classroom;

- changing dressing-up clothes or objects in the home corner to suggest new play scenarios;

- providing suitcases for various characters from a storybook to suggest that they might be going on holiday or about to arrive in the classroom.

Playing with adults

Play can increase motivation and boost self-esteem because, during it, children experiment and test hypotheses without fear of failure. Above all, they can try out imaginative and original ways of solving problems without interference from adults. Nevertheless, sensitive interventions are crucial to expanding the creative potential of play as they encourage children to think about what they are doing as they try to reach a solution or a decision. For example, understanding a sequence of events relating to an exciting event in a child's life, such as an outing or a party, can be deepened when adults ask 'What happened first?', 'What followed next?' and 'How did it all end up?'. Such events could become a play scenario if, for example, a child's bedroom, or the home corner (if it is in school) is turned into a museum where artefacts such as old teddies are put on view to stimulate curiosity and playful response. Adults can ask children to think about how the teddy bears got there, whose they are, or how they should be displayed. Creative play provides opportunities for children to 'revisit' a significant event and so deepen their understanding of that experience.

Much is known about the importance of preschool influences on the emergence of literacy.[5] Family play activities provide a context for learning through familiar everyday experiences in an environment where the child feels safe to experiment and make mistakes. The learning potential of an activity is enhanced when parents or carers interact with children in supportive ways that encourage the child to think creatively. Intervention may take the form of asking and answering questions that provoke deeper levels of thinking and understanding. This can be as simple as discussing with young children what they might do at playschool or nursery in the morning. Discussion with adults that draws on what they know and have can provide the oral groundwork for future literacy, providing a sound foundation on which to build their understanding of how to read and write.

Stories derived from personal experience, from reading books or from drawing, offer good starting points for children to create their own spoken stories. Children delight in hearing of the childhood experiences of adults, for example stories about their schooldays or holidays in the past, and comparing these with their own. Young children should also be encouraged to tell their own stories, perhaps continuing one that an adult has started for them. As storywriting most closely mirrors spoken language, it will be easier for children to compose stories as they can use words and phrases and story forms they have already heard. If adults have modelled the sequence of story events, as above, children can appreciate the need to provide beginnings, middles and endings that are sequential. Once they have imaginatively played with these forms, children can write about their own experiences – for instance, 'My first day at school' or 'When I got lost in the airport' – in a more confident and compelling manner.

Children should be introduced to commercially produced games in the home that have a direct educational purpose such as word jigsaw puzzles or 'sounds' dominoes. Playing games in which adults take the lead, such as in 'I-Spy' or 'Simon says' helps to develop phonemic awareness (the ability to hear individual sounds in words) and short-term memory. They also provide opportunities for creative wordplay, such as word-morphing, where one word is changed into another by changing one letter, e.g. 'cat' → 'can' → 'man', or by finding a rhyme.

Play serves many purposes, but for young children it is often an end in itself. It can involve participants in complex levels of thinking as they interpret and reinterpret experiences and share them with one another child and/or adults. It is during the reformulation of experience through thinking that deeper understanding is developed.[6]

23

Learning through play at school

Active approaches to learning, like those in the home, should also be offered in Early Years educational settings such as playgroups, nurseries and Key Stage 1 classrooms. In the *Curriculum Guidance for the Foundation Stage* (2000: 27) play is seen as both a context for children's learning as well as a means of keeping motivation high, for 'well-planned play, both indoors and outdoors, is a key way in which young children learn with enjoyment and challenge'.

In the UK, the Foundation Stage is for children between the ages of 3 and 5, but by Early Years we include Key Stage 1 pupils in state schools, so it encompasses children aged from 3 to 7. Research shows that young children learn best where the learning potential of play is fully appreciated and suggests that it is counterproductive to start formal learning too soon because children learn best in ways that are holistic and context-specific.[7] During play activity the child creates a world that has a reality of its own, and this is beneficial. But to have real purpose it needs to be carefully planned.

To ensure that play is purposeful, it should be challenging, so that children are encouraged to think deeply and learn to persevere while engaging in creative and stimulating activities. Imagination needs to be fostered through probing questioning while they engage in intellectually stimulating activities.[8] One-to-one dialogue can help to mediate understanding, such as when adults respond to what children are doing and/or saying by asking them:

- 'Do you mean that . . .?';
- 'I think I understand what you are saying. You think that . . .?';
- 'Remember when we looked at . . .'; and
- 'What would happen if . . .?'

Children can be helped to solve problems if they are challenged to think about solutions in terms of:

- 'How does that help?';
- 'What else do you need to think about?'; and
- 'Can you think of another way of doing that?'

They can be challenged to explore new objects or ideas when prompted to think creatively about them in terms of:

- 'Does it remind you of anything?';
- 'Have you done anything like that before?'; and
- 'What does it smell (taste, feel, look or sound) like?'

Adults are sometimes reluctant to intervene in children's play because they are afraid that they will disrupt the imaginative flow, but high levels of interaction involving questioning and the recall and reformulation of ideas by the child will enhance its quality. Through questioning children can be encouraged to be creative and imaginative by being asked to analyse what did or did not work. Creative learning occurs best when children engage in challenging dialogues with adults (and each other) during the process of solving problems or investigating new objects or ideas; for example by discussing why some objects float while others sink, or social issues, such as why bullying is unacceptable behaviour.

The adult's role in this dialogue is to ask challenging questions that:

- make appropriate cognitive demands – making the task neither too easy nor too difficult;
- manage the response – by bringing aspects of partial learning together;
- help the child to see a task/problem through sequentially;
- help the child to select appropriate materials;
- check that the child's response is appropriate;
- keep the child *actively* involved;
- pace questions asked, so that an appropriate number of challenging questions are posed – neither too many nor too few; and
- give a shape to session – by drawing the threads of learning and understanding together in a plenary.

(adapted from Meadows and Cashdan 1988)

Creative literacy learning

Once children start school they will be taught literacy through a curriculum such as the Programmes of Study of the English National Curriculum (1999). If children's levels of motivation are to remain high they need to be taught in inspirational, playful and stimulating ways where time for gestation of ideas and collaboration with each other provide the support for early success.

Speaking and listening

Playing together gives children the opportunity to experiment with speaking and listening as they try out their language repertoire on one another. Play allows them to use language for a number of purposes, as well as giving them understanding of how other people use it. They need to become aware that people use spoken language in ways that are:

- instrumental (getting something done, e.g. *I want*);
- regulatory (where control is exercised, e.g. *Go to sleep*);

- interactional (to achieve group membership/acceptability, e.g. *Can I play with you?*);

- personal (all about me, e.g. *I am tired*);

- heuristic (as a means of investigating reality by asking questions, e.g. *Why?*, *What?*, *Where?* etc.);

- imaginative (attempting to create something not yet experienced, e.g. *Let's pretend*); and

- representational (words stand for something already experienced, e.g. *We went to see my nan in hospital*)

(adapted from Halliday, 1978)

As they plan their imaginative games together, children have to decide what the beginning, the middle and the end might be: an ordering activity that may help them when they start to plan their writing. Through speaking and listening in imaginary play situations children develop communicative competence, including understanding the conventions for successful dialogue, such as turn-taking and the need to build upon what has been said before. Role-play sessions enable children to respond to each other when they become characters from a story, for example a Viking raider or King Cnut, or the harassed residents of Hamelin (in the story of the Pied Piper), or a nursery rhyme character like Little Bo Peep distressed at the loss of her sheep. Telling anecdotes from real-life experience can also offer useful starting points for writing.[9] An example of this is found in the following extract from a poem written by Allan Ahlberg, where making up excuses takes an unexpected and far-fetched turn:

Excuses

> *I've writ on the wrong page, Miss.*
> *My pencil went all blunt.*
> *My book was upside-down, Miss.*
> *My book was back to front.*

The excuses become increasingly more preposterous until they reach this incredulous climax in the final verse:

> *I've ate a poison apple, Miss.*
> *I've held a poison pen!*
> *I think I'm being kidnapped, Miss!*
> *So . . . can we start again?*

Everyday situations, as in the poem above, are made more enjoyable when they take a leap in to the unreal, for example in the story *Not Now, Bernard* by David McKee where a little boy who fails to gain the attention of his parents resorts to pretending that he has been eaten by a monster, still to no avail.

Children who are shy can gain in confidence in speaking by becoming the mouth-piece for a puppet. This puts less strain on them and allows them to communicate ideas while adopting another persona. Puppet plays provide endless opportunities for verbal creativity – as the long tradition of Punch and Judy displays. Children need the opportunity to invent stories orally before attempting to write their ideas down. Oral composition can be used to generate ideas. If used effectively it enables children to:

- keep the story in their heads, giving them a clear sense of what they hope to achieve in the whole text;

- establish the style and voice of the particular piece of writing they are undertaking;

- sequence and structure their writing to provide cohesion and to ensure that it makes sense; and

- establish a reference point that keeps the writing on track.

(NLS 2001)

In the early stages of developing literacy, adults should help children to remember their 'oral' plans and encourage them to be imaginative by asking them challenging questions such as, 'What might happen next?' or 'What strange/scary/surprising/exciting event might happen in your story?'

Reading

Research shows that young children who have had their attention drawn to print in the environment around them come to know that printed words convey meaning and that books have stories to tell. Where story readings become a daily occurrence, such as at bedtime, some important aspects of the reading process will be learned.[10] For example, through several readings of favourite stories children realise that language becomes permanent once it has been printed and that words remain the same every time the book is read to them.[11] Children will often pretend they are reading before they can do so correctly. I once observed a small child singing carols in a local supermarket just before Christmas. She was holding up an advertising leaflet, just as you would a hymn-book in church, and singing for all she was worth! Children frequently adopt creative reading-like behaviour like this, often concentrating initially on the pictures in the book, in a bid to gain meaning from the text. As their experiences of books increases they come to better understand the message contained in the print. Each act of reading becomes a re-creation of the first experience of the story. Woe betide the adult who through momentary loss of concentration, alters the text in any way when reading a familiar story!

From such encounters with texts children start to recognise frequently recurring words, both in and out of context. Gradually they are able to make increasing sense of the actual words on the page, and know how these are combined to form sentences. They begin to make creative predictions about what unknown words should be, based on the context of the story and knowledge of the syntax of English. These early experiences with text, taking place primarily for enjoyment, provide children with opportunities to learn strategies that will help them process the many new words they will encounter as they become older.

Through the repetition of stories, rhymes, jingles and poems, they learn the sounds of language and ultimately gain phonemic awareness of the individual phonemes in words. Wordplay can help in this process, for example games such as:

- 'I hear with my little ear something that rhymes with "hat" ';
- alliterative games using children's names as the starting point, e.g. 'Mary munches Mars bars, David drinks dandelion wine';
- 'My name begins with . . ., my mum's name begins with . . ., my brother/sister's name begins with . . .'; and
- 'The farmer's cow has . . .' (with each suggestion starting with a phoneme selected by the teacher or a specially chosen child).

Multisensory games can be played; for example, trying to make the shape of letters and words in the air or tracing how they feel on cards with the letter shapes raised on them in stuck-on sand. Research has shown that children as young as three or four years of age are able to distinguish between the different phonemes in words by playing odd-one-out games in which they are able to hear the difference between the medial phonemes (middle sounds) in 'pin, bin, gun'.[12] This emphasises the value of creative word play with young children. Problem-solving techniques, such as how to make analogies from a known word to one that is unknown can provide creative solutions to reading unfamiliar words.[13] For example, if a child can read 'cake', she should be able to read 'make' and 'take' by recognising that each of these words has the same rime (the part of the syllable that contains the vowel, or vowel digraph, and final consonant or consonant cluster) and that only the initial phoneme has changed.

To enable children to gain deeper meaning from texts they can be encouraged to think creatively by using their imaginations to play out the themes from stories in the home corner which can be turned into the set for a favourite story; for example Little Red Riding Hood's grandmother's cottage. Imaginative play areas (or themes) are essential for every Early Years classroom. They need to be planned as carefully as any other aspect of learning. For instance, children could go on a Bear Hunt (Rosen and Oxenbury 1989) following a carefully prepared written trail. The provision of appropriate reading material in the home corner, such as magazines, brochures and telephone directories, can encourage children to try to read for themselves.

Older children can grapple with complex ideas in texts through drama, for example 'fear' or 'the supernatural'. Understanding of these can be gained through discussion of role play aimed at finding creative solutions to problems raised, such as what possessions to take into hiding, as in the case of Anne Frank. Children can cope with the challenging dialogues contained in Shakespeare by working together in creative ways on carefully chosen passages like *Macbeth* Act 1, Scene 1: The Three Witches, where children can be asked to provide a 'soundscape' of what it would be like on the 'blasted heath' (Johnson, in Fisher and Williams 2000).

Writing

Children's earliest creative attempts at mark-making are often systematic and logical.[14] They need to be given opportunities to write for themselves, or to have their writing scribed by willing adults, as they attempt to compose their own letters or stories or to make lists of things they need or want. As a child I used to write sermons like my dad, including underlining the points that needed emphasis in red ink, just as he did, although to the outside eye this was nothing more than a series of joined-up squiggles on the page. By including writing in their play children develop awareness of key principles about writing as they try to make sense of what they are doing. They make creative hypotheses about the process as they engage in it for themselves. As one child said of her particular mark-making, 'I don't need to write much – it's only a postcard'.

Children's understanding of written genres can be extended through writing in role in the home corner. It can become Postman Pat's post office or the Three Bears' cottage. They can write, for example, a letter from the Three Bears to Goldilocks's parents to express concern about the damage she caused to their home. The following reply was written by a six-year-old boy. His 'creative' spellings have been corrected, although they were all phonetically plausible, but the punctuation is his own.

Dear Mr and Mrs Gold

We are very very cross with your daughter. She broke our son's chair and ate his porridge and dirtied his bed. No! We dont like it. She didn't even say sorry. We are angry. Baby bear is putting his tears everywhere.

The Bears

This letter shows that he is already able to 'construct and convey meaning in written language matching style to audience and purpose' (DES 1989 : 17.34), the main objective for the National Curriculum attainment target for writing. He had been given a meaningful context for his writing through sharing the *Jolly Postman and Other Stories* by Allan and Janet Ahlberg and knew about letter-writing from writing 'thank you' letters following his birthday. Also, he had an interesting problem to solve that gave him a creative reason for writing, and a sense of the audience he was writing for.

As children become older they need to be given challenges that broaden their repertoire for writing to include functional forms that serve practical purposes. They should be encouraged to write:

- signs and posters to publicise events;
- labels and captions for drawings or models;

- lists of what they need to do, or to collect, to undertake certain tasks;
- instructions about how to play a game or how an object can be made to work;
- accounts of events that have happened to them; and
- reports of experiments, or conclusions reached as part of problem-solving activities.[15]

These can take place in the home corner, for example as they write menus when it is a café, shopping lists when it is a supermarket or posters publicising a puppet show.

Eventually, they will need to be able to write creatively across the genres of non-fiction that include the following:

- a recount, e.g. of a visit to a theme park;
- a report, e.g. of a special event that has taken place in school like the visit of a famous children's author;
- an explanation, e.g. of how people used to wash clothes before there were washing-machines;
- instruction, e.g. of how to play a board game they have made based on the Harry Potter stories;
- persuasion to a point of view, e.g. that children should be permitted to go to bed when they like;
- discussion revealing the pros and cons of an argument about whether, e.g., children should decide what they want to eat for themselves.

(Wray and Lewis 1997)

Writing frames can be very useful for introducing these styles, but their creativity will be stifled if their experience of writing is limited to writing frames or worksheets.

Children need to become familiar with the creative process of writing in which the various stages they go through – plan, draft, edit, revise – are seen as important learning opportunities, as much as the created product, as most great literary works go through many drafts.

In summary, play can provide creative opportunities for literacy development either at home or in school in many ways. These can include:

- games that draw on environmental print, such as reading billboards and road signs to prevent boredom on long car journeys, or through the print-rich environment found in many classrooms where walls are festooned with labelled work and charts that provide 'real' contexts for reading and writing;
- word games, sounds games, and learning songs and rhymes that increase phonemic awareness, such as nursery and action rhymes;
- commercially produced games such as Junior Scrabble, where concepts about letters and words can be developed; letter games or jigsaws that make the learning of

the alphabet enjoyable and provide a context for knowing both graphemes and phonemes. The reciprocal nature of these verbal exchanges also helps children appreciate the social conventions of conversation;

■ word games or activities that encourage a 'play on words' and develop awareness that language has more than one meaning, such as games that require that the correct homograph is used in the right place by holding up the appropriate word card as a story is told, for example, 'the *knight* in shining armour set out on a moonlit *night* to find . . .';

■ having stories or poems read to them for entertainment purposes, motivating them to read for themselves and encouraging them to own favourite books. Equally, themes from books or poems read at bedtime, or as classroom story-time favourites, can inspire them to become authors themselves;

■ gaining factual information by being given access to information texts, including CD-ROMs that satisfy and feed children's natural curiosity about the world;

■ creating oral and written plans for the plot of an imaginative play theme, or character sketches in preparation for a puppet play. These will aid children's ability to plan their writing. Making labels for the scenery in plays or for displays for the classroom that increase understanding of the descriptive power of language;

■ imaginative role play that involves writing for a specific purpose; for instance sets of instructions or the props needed for a play theme that provide a reason for engaging in non-fiction writing, or writing as part of the play itself; for example, writing a menu for a café as the chef, or a prescription in the role of a doctor;

■ encouraging children to do 'homework' or to attempt to read books like older siblings, as it is known that useful role models can be provided by older pupils in school through cross-peer tutoring programmes in reading and writing.[16]

Learning to learn

Recent research has shown that children are able to become metacognitively aware of how they think and learn from an early age and that this enhances the quality of their learning.[17] Metacognitive awareness is gained through reflection about how the learning has occurred, enabling children to achieve deeper understanding of what is involved. It helps them to be consciously aware of how to think about similar challenges in the future, so that their thinking becomes more self-directed.

Metacognitive awareness helps them to know what is going on in their minds while they engage creatively in carrying out literacy tasks. For instance, a six-year-old boy revealed his growing understanding of the writing process when he said: 'If you couldn't write, you couldn't write a word, if you didn't know how to learn, like when you was young'.

Teachers need to enter into challenging dialogues with children in order to get inside their thinking, by getting them to share their understanding of what they know or what they think to be the case. With young children metacognitive awareness begins by helping children to become more aware of how they are thinking while engaged in practical tasks.

Questions to generate awareness of how to solve literacy problems creatively:

- How do you know that?

- How did you figure that out?

- What evidence do you have for that?

- Are there some words in the story that make you think that?

- Can you think of another way of working that out?

- Can you think of another word that means that?

- Do you think that sounds right?

- Will the same happen if you do it again?

Metacognition is enhanced by having a shared language with which to talk about various aspects of the literacy process. Young children do not shy away from learning relevant terminology as long as it is taught through contexts that have meaning for them. Children need to be able to use language to discuss language[18] and to think about how they think. For example, one young child used this analogy to explain what her memory was for: 'It is like a dictionary we have in our own minds, when we try to find the words we've forgotten'.

Asking children *why* they know something to be the case challenges their thinking and awareness. In the early stages adults act as mediators for children's learning through a two-way process in which the learner and teacher make meaning through dialogue in which the adult depends on the child as much as the other way round; for example, when the teacher needs to know what a child understands in order to plan effectively for the future, or when a child reveals partial understanding that necessitates a new approach to learning.[19] It is through free-flowing verbal exchanges that cognitive understanding is transformed, as new insights develop and metacognitive awareness increases. This is often achieved when adults play *with* children, sharing a particular context with them that has significance for them both. If children know how they have learned something, they are more likely to make creative and conscious decisions about whether to use similar strategies in the future. An example of this was a child who said, 'I know what to do cos I've worked it out before!'

Young children may show signs of being metacognitively aware through play activities before they enter formal schooling. Recent research with gifted and talented children in Year 1 (five- to six-year-olds) showed that these children already had some metacognitive understanding of how they were learning to be literate.[20] This included knowing that:

- a systematic approach to learning can be useful with Mark cataloguing his comics so that he could easily look up favourite topics in the future;

- phonemic and phonic knowledge are important aspects of learning to read, e.g. Craig who was able to use his knowledge of the rime 'ock' in 'clock' to read 'block' and was able to tell the researcher that this was what he was doing;

- words contain syllables, and that this helps when it comes to reading and writing, e.g. David said that he put his finger in the middle of words he could not read and this sometimes helped him 'to think up the first word, then the second', showing that he had growing understanding that some words are compound;

- reading fiction and non-fiction books differs, e.g. Mark who knew that he could gain information from books about subjects he was interested in, as well as delighting in having stories read to him; and

- being literate is empowering so, as David said, 'you can read to your children when you are a daddy'.

In addition, Mark (whose comments head up this chapter) already knew that he needed to captivate his audience when he writes. His dad reported that 'he writes in order to get a response from his audience. He wants you to read it and wants you to know what his thoughts are and before you can even get a chance to read it, he tells you what he has written.'

Above all, metacognitive awareness had helped these children to realise *why* it is important to be able to read and write. As a result they were able to discuss their own learning strategies and to approach learning in creative, problem-solving ways. This gave them the motivation to acquire greater understanding and skills in literacy.

Conclusion

In summary, children can learn to be literate creatively through play that can be divided into several types:

- structured games and activities;
- informal games that form part of family life;
- play or literacy activities inspired by story or poetry readings;
- planning for imaginative play; and
- play motivated by emulating siblings.

(Williams 2003)

Learning through play needs to be mediated by adults who help children acquire the knowledge, skills and understanding they need to make sense of the world around them. In literacy terms, play allows children to develop understanding of the purposes and power of the written word through discovery, hypothesis-raising and experimentation, and they are unlikely to achieve this without the interventions of supportive and question-asking adults. Above all, play gives children the opportunity to learn in 'meaningful' contexts that give them a sense of audience and purpose for what they are doing. More than this, it is a valuable means of challenging them to think creatively by helping them to develop awareness of how they think and learn.

Within the context of the National Curriculum and the National Literacy Strategy in the UK, it is essential that motivation for literacy learning remains high. The best teachers take a flexible and creative approach to the Literacy Hour.

Time for 'purposeful' play needs to be found in formal settings, as young children benefit from being given opportunities to learn through play. It enables them to experience literacy in creative and interesting ways. Play also provides a means through which children's metacognitive awareness of how they are learning can be developed, through discussion about how they know something, as well as what they know and what they can do with what they know. Such awareness will help them to make creative decisions about how to tackle literacy tasks in the future and become more independent orally, and in reading and writing. This, in turn, will help them to lead creative, stimulating lives.

Notes

1 Williams and Rask (2000) define play and look at the ways in which higher-ability children in Year 1 extend and develop their literacy skills through play.

2 Bruce (1991) considers the nature of play and discusses how it can be either free-flowing or more structured.

3 Early Years educators such as Montessori (1870–1952), Froebel (1782–1852) and Issacs (1885–1948) have stamped their mark on the type of education that is offered today to young children in both formal and informal settings. More recently, writers such as Browne (1996), Fisher (1996) and David (1998) have researched how young children learn in the Early Years.

4 Hall and Robinson, in Barratt-Pugh and Rohl (2000), explore the links between play and literacy.

5 Clark (1976), Wells (1986), Athey (1990), Weinberger (1996), Marsh and Hallet (1999) have all attested to the positive benefits of preschool literacy activities on language and literacy learning.

6 Vygotsky (1986) wrote about the close relationship between thought and language.

7 Bruce (1991), Moyles (1994), Anning (1997), Hall and Abbott (1991) write about the learning potential of play.

8 Nutbrown (1999) considers how children think and learn about the world.

9 Rosen (1989) explored the role of anecdotes in 'Did I Hear You Write?'

10 Holdaway (1979) outlined the importance of the bedtime cycle in *The Foundations of Literacy*. He has been a major influence behind approaches offered in the Literacy Hour during shared reading and writing.

11 Clay (1979) realised that children's earliest mark-making was much more than mere scribbling.

12 Bradley and Bryant (1983) and Adams (1990) have researched into young children's awareness of phonemes and how they acquire phonic knowledge.

13 Goswami (1999) showed that analogy making forms an important part of young children's acquisition of phonic knowledge.

14 Clay (1979), Ferrerio and Teberosky (1979) and Hall (1987) discuss how children develop principles about the writing process from an early age.

15 Williams outlined functional forms of writing in Fisher, R. and Williams, M. (eds) (2000) *Unlocking Literacy*. London: David Fulton.

16 Topping (2001) has written extensively about children learning through paired reading and writing programmes in which older, or similar aged pupils, act as their tutors in school.

17 Fisher (1998), Williams (2000), Williams and Rask (2000), Topping (2001) and Guterman (2002) have researched the role of metacognition in literacy learning.

18 Wray (1994) considers that children need to know a technical language in order to discuss their literacy learning effectively.

19 Souza (2001) has written about the dynamic relationship that exists between adult and child as they talk about aspects of learning, with both learning from each other.

20 Williams and Rask (2000).

Further reading

Adams, M. (1990) *Beginning to Read*. London: Heinemann.

Anning, A. (1997) *The First Years of Schooling* (2nd edn). Buckingham: Open University Press.

Athey, C. (1990) *Extending Thought in Young Children*. London: Paul Chapman.

Barratt-Pugh, C. and Rohl, M. (eds) (2000) *Literacy Learning in the Early Years*. Buckingham: Open University Press.

Bradley, L. and Bryant, P. (1983) 'Categorising sounds and learning to read: a causal connection'. *Nature*, 310, 419–21.

Browne, A. (1996) *Developing Language and Literacy*. London: Paul Chapman.

Bruce, T. (1991) *Time to Play*. London: Hodder & Stoughton.

Clark, M. (1976) *Young Fluent Readers*. London: Heinemann.

Clay, M. (1979) *Reading: The Patterning of Complex Behaviour* (2nd edn). London: Heinemann.

David, T. (1998) 'Learning properly! Young children and desirable outcomes'. *Journal of the Professional Association of Early Childhood Educators*, 18(2), Spring.

DES (1989) *English for Ages 5–16*. York: NCC.

DfEE (1996) *Desirable Outcomes for Children's Learning*. London: HMSO.

DfEE (1998) *The National Literacy Strategy*. London: Sanctuary Buildings.

DfEE (1999), *Early Learning Goals*, London: Sanctuary Buildings.

DfEE (1999) *The National Curriculum Handbook for Primary/Secondary Teachers in England & Wales*. London: DfEE.

Ferreiro, E. and Teberosky, A. (1979) *Literacy Before Schooling*. London: Heinemann.

Fisher, J. (1996) *Starting from the Child*. Buckingham: Open University Press.

Fisher, R. (1998) 'Thinking about thinking: developing metacognition in children'. *Early Child Development and Care*, 141, 1–13.

Fisher, R. (2002) 'Shared thinking: metacognitive modelling in the Literacy Hour'. *Reading*, 36(2), July.

Fisher, R. and Williams, M. (eds) (2000) *Unlocking Literacy*. London: David Fulton.

Goswami, U. (1999) 'Causal connections in beginning reading: the importance of rhyme'. *Journal of Research in Reading*, 22(3), October, 217–40.

Guterman, E. (2002) 'Towards dynamic assessment of reading: applying metacognitive awareness guidance to reading assessment'. *Journal of Research in Reading*, 25(3), 283–98.

Hall, N. (1987) *The Emergence of Literacy*. London: Hodder & Stoughton.

Hall, N. and Abbott, L. (1991) *Playing in the Primary Classroom*. London: Hodder & Stoughton.

Hall, N. and Robinson, A. (2000) 'Play and literacy learning', in Barratt-Pugh, C. and Rohl, M. (eds) (2000) *Literacy Learning in the Early Years*. Buckingham: Open University Press.

Halliday, M. (1978) *Language as a Social Semiotic*. London: Edward Arnold.

Holdaway, D. (1979) 'The foundations of literacy'. London: Aston Scholastic.

Johnson, C. (2000) 'What did I say?: speaking, listening and drama', in Fisher, R. and Williams, M. *Unlocking Literacy*. London: David Fulton.

Marsh, J. and Hallet, E. (1999) *Desirable Literacies*. London: Paul Chapman.

Meadows, C. and Cashdan, A. (1988) *Helping Children Learning*. London: David Fulton.

Meek, M. (1991) *On Being Literate*. London: Bodley Head.

Moyles, J. (ed.) (1994) *The Excellence of Play*. Buckingham: Open University Press.

NLS (2001) *Developing Early Writing*. London: DfEE.

Nutbrown, C. (1999) *Threads of Thinking* (2nd edn). London: Paul Chapman.

QCA (2000) *Curriculum Guidance for the Foundation Stage*. London: DfEE.

Quirke, J. and Winter, C. (1994) 'Teaching the language of learning'. *British Educational Research Journal*, 20 (4).

Rosen, M. (1989) *Did I Hear You Write?* London: Andre Deutsch.

Souza, J. and S. (2001) 'The construction of contemporary subjectivity: interactions between knowledge and school environs', in Hedegaard, M. *Learning in Classrooms*. Aarhus, Denmark: Aarhus University Press.

Topping, K. (2001) *Thinking Reading Writing*. London: Continuum.

Vygotsky, L. (1986) *Thought and Language*. Cambridge, Mass.: MIT Press.

Weinberger, J. (1996) *Literacy Goes to School*. London: Paul Chapman.

Wells, G. (1986) *The Meaning Makers*. London: Hodder & Stoughton.

Williams, M. (2000) 'The part which metacognition can play in raising standards in English at Key Stage 2'. *Reading*, 34(1), April.

Williams, M. (2000) 'Playing with words', in Fisher, R. and Williams, M. *Unlocking Literacy*. London: David Fulton.

Williams, M. (ed.) (2002) *Unlocking Writing*. London: David Fulton.

Williams, M. (2003) 'The importance of metacognition in the literacy development of young gifted and talented children'. *Gifted Education International*, 17 (3), Autumn, 249–58.

Williams, M. and Rask, H. (2000) 'The identification of variables which enable children in year one to extend and develop their literacy skills'. *Gifted and Talented*, 4 (2), November, 29–35.

Wray, D. (1994) *Literacy and Awareness*. London: Hodder & Stoughton.

Wray, D. and Lewis, M. (1997) *Extending Literacy: Children Reading and Writing Non Fiction*. London: Routledge.

Children's literature/resources

Allan Ahlberg (1984) *Please Mrs. Butler*. Harmondsworth: Puffin.

Allan and Janet Ahlberg (1986) *The Jolly Postman or Other People's Letters*. London: Heinemann.

David McKee (1980) *Not Now, Bernard*. London: Anderson Press.

Rosen, M. and Oxenbury, H. (1989) *We're Going on a Bear Hunt*. London: Walker Books.

Creative writing: taking risks with words

Andrew Green

Introduction

IN *THE LITERARY WORLD* Philip Larkin, in characteristically wry fashion, observes:

I

'Finally, after five months of my life during which I could write nothing that would have satisfied me, and for which no power will compensate me . . .'

My dear Kafka,
When you've had five years of it, not five months,
Five years of an irresistible force meeting an
immoveable object right in your belly,
Then you'll know about depression.

II

Mrs Alfred Tennyson
Answered
begging letters
admiring letters
insulting letters
enquiring letters
business letters
and publishers' letters.
She also
looked after his clothes
saw to his food and drink
entertained visitors
protected him from gossip and criticism
And finally
(apart from running the household)
Brought up and educated the children.

> While all this was going on
> Mister Alfred Tennyson sat like a baby
> Doing his poetic business.

This poem outlines two contrasting but equally stereotypical views of the artist and the relationship between the author and his work. The first emphasises the pain and the sometimes fruitless work involved in the process of poetic creation – the conventional tortured author with writer's block; while the second paints a humorously disengaged portrait of the Romantic poet floating through life in undisturbed creative oblivion. Neither is, perhaps, a particularly helpful stereotype, but Larkin's poem serves neatly to outline two of the most common perceptions of creativity and the creative artist.[1]

This chapter focuses upon the ways in which creative writing is perceived and the myths that so often exist around it. It looks to establish clearly what may be understood by the term creativity within the context of writing, exploring a number of manifestations of creativity. The connections between reading, writing and creativity are explored with practical applications to ways creativity can be encouraged in pupils through the careful and sensitive teaching of processes of writing.

The myth of the creative artist

Every writer – good or bad, young or old, professional or amateur – lives in the shadow of greatness. The evidence is all around us: *Kubla Khan* was, Coleridge claimed, written in the white heat of an opium-induced dream; *Frankenstein*, one of the most influential novels of all time, was astonishingly produced by the nineteen- year-old Mary Shelley; *On the Road*, Jack Kerouac's masterpiece, was written in a frenzied three weeks of inspiration; and then we may go on to consider the extensive works of such undisputed masters as Shakespeare, T.S. Eliot and Charles Dickens. How did they do it? What was their inspiration? How did they attain their mastery of language, form and powers of narrative? How could they create such characters? It is no wonder that, for many, the process of writing is intimidating.

It is perhaps because of this that a mythology springs up around great creative artists. They exist in ivory towers of the imagination, in a rarefied world of letters; they stalk the streets of Paris or Prague or London in dreamworlds of creation, or live out lives of frugal and romantic isolation in garrets for the sake of their art. The artist becomes an artistic creation of the popular imagination, set apart from the rest of humanity. Because of this popular myth, not only the creative artist, but also creativity itself and the talents associated with it, are set up on a pedestal, the preserve of the select few.

And yet it is the very same act of 'creation' that we demand of children in the sometimes cramped, occasionally insalubrious and frequently time-pressured environment of the classroom. On a daily basis, pupils in their English lessons are expected to participate in creative activities using the written word – activities involving them in highly personal and often experimental work, where creative learning and development need to escape banks of objectives and to move into the numinous relationship between the author, the written word and the reader. The role of the teacher in building stimulating and appropriate environments within which such creativity can flourish is central, especially in the increasingly pressured environment of the classroom, where creation on demand is often required.

Writing is work

For the majority of authors, including many of the most famous artists the world has known, the reality of writing is rather different from the stereotypical notion of the inspired and frenzied act of artistic creation. Too often the fact that a work of art is inspirational is enough for it to be considered as the work of inspired genius, and this encourages a skewed view of the true nature of the writing experience. Quite at odds with this view of the creative spirit, Thomas Edison once famously claimed that genius is 'one percent inspiration and ninety-nine percent perspiration', reversing the popular myth of the genius as some kind of elevated vessel through whom inspiration passes and emerges as the 'work of art'. Edison, a pragmatist and a lifelong believer in the ethic of hard work, recognised that inspiration alone can count for no great work of creation. Creative productions are, after all, known as *works* of art. Initial inspiration there must be for any creative or original theory, discovery, piece of writing, painting, sculpture or musical composition, but once the inspiration has come the work begins. Charles Dickens was known for the phenomenal rate of his writing, at one time working simultaneously on the manuscripts of *Nicholas Nickelby* and *Oliver Twist*, one in the mornings and the other in the afternoons, while another of the great Victorian novelists, Anthony Trollope, who is also acknowledged as the founder of the first organised postal system, wrote to a strict regime, and even fashioned a desk to sit across his horse's neck so that he could write while travelling on postal business.

Inspiration alone does not account for all of creativity. Mozart was able to produce his final three symphonies in a mere seven weeks, and in the short span of his 35 years produced a vast amount of music of the highest quality. At the other extreme, however, Gustave Flaubert, the French novelist, would work for a day to perfect just one sentence, and James Joyce took 22 years to complete his controversial masterpiece *Finnegan's Wake*. The process of writing, even for the genius, is not always easy, but it involves a healthy amount of plain hard work.

Reading and creative writing

Debra Myhill has observed that 'Learning to write is at once one of the most commonplace and one of the most complex activities we ask children to undertake in school'.[2] Writing lies at the very heart of the child's school experience. The ability effectively to create with the written word in a wide variety of forms and for an ever-widening range of purposes is central to the child's personal and intellectual development. The written word, rightly or wrongly, is also the foremost method of assessment under the current system in all areas of the curriculum, and, as such, pupils need to learn to function creatively in the written media.

To be fully creative in their engagement with the act of writing, however, creative response to written text as readers is also essential. It has become something of a platitude to observe that the way to become an effective writer and to develop a mastery of the complexities of writing is to read 'good' examples of such writing. This, however, is not an unproblematic assertion and it is important to evaluate the nature of the relationship between the read word and the written word. Gunther Kress, identifies the fundamental connection between reading and writing, observing:

> Reading and writing are functionally differentiated aspects of one system, and of one set of processes. An exclusive concern with either overlooks essential characteristics shared by both. Most importantly, reading and writing are both activities that draw on the forms, structures and processes of language in its written mode . . . Hence neither the process of reading nor that of writing can be understood in isolation from the other.[3]

Let us consider what this implies. It posits a symbiotic relationship between the processes of reading and writing. An eclectic and avid reader will have a fuller frame of reference and a greater potential conceptualisation of the possibilities of the written word and the means by which authors seek to convey meaning and to influence their readers. Conversely, the more limited the reading experience of an individual the less they will bring to their own writing by way of such experience. These factors impact upon the pupil's ability as a writer in a number of ways in terms of:

- form and structure;
- syntax and vocabulary;
- the ability to read and critically evaluate their own writing; and
- the ability to respond to generic features and techniques.

Kress suggests that the success of the individual as a writer cannot be separated from their success as a reader; that the possession of skills in one area will necessarily transpose onto the other. He assumes no simple connection between the two, however. The act of reading itself cannot somehow lead to an osmotic transfer of ability from reading into writing. The reality is rather less clear-cut, as identified in a recent DfES publication: 'In spite of improvements at Key Stages 1, 2 and 3 over the past three years, standards of writing, and particularly boys' writing, remain lower than standards of reading'.[4]

Kress, too, highlights this in describing the two processes as 'functionally differentiated'. They are two sides of the same coin – fundamentally attached, but facing in different directions.

The act of reading introduces the reader to language in action and opens the potential for engagement with it, but it is only with structured guidance that such contact can be converted into the true engagement that broadens the reader's knowledge of language at work and deepens understanding of the potential of the written word. With appropriate teacher input, such as questions to provoke discussion of text, the exploration of authorial choices at word, sentence and text level; and the provision of differentiated reading support; the young reader can be enabled to approach and evaluate the ways in which writers achieve certain effects and the impact that these can have, thus providing a set of tools that can be used to emulate the effect. Such an approach is the technique of Guided Reading advocated by the National Strategy. The process is necessarily complex, however, and can never lead to a straightforward assimilation of knowledge and/or technique. It is even possible that the act of reading can lead to a crisis of confidence in the writer, whereby the proliferation of surrounding authorial voices becomes an inhibition to individual creativity.

Bloom's *The Anxiety of Influence*: creativity or originality?

In this work, a theory of poetic development, Harold Bloom identifies a series of six stages through which a writer develops, all of which are conceived in terms of a direct relation with other writings, or models.[5] These he terms as follows:

TABLE 3.1 Bloom's six stages of the writer's development

clinamen	poetic misreading or misprision: the identification of weakness or incompletion in the model
tessera	completion and antithesis: an attempt to 'complete' or make up the deficiency in the model
kenosis	a movement to discontinuity: a positive move away from the model, and advance into individualism
daemonisation	a movement to personalisation: the initial recognition and formation of an individual 'voice'
askesis	self-purgation: full movement away from the model
apophrades	the return of the dead: mastery of the individual 'voice' and the appropriation of the model.

Although a simplification of Bloom's complex hypothesis, this provides a useful starting point from which to approach writerly assimilation and the development of the creative 'voice'. Few writers will go on to develop a wholly individual voice, but the stages of development Bloom outlines can usefully be applied to the three different facets of creativity Robert Fisher identifies in Chapter 1: creativity as generation; creativity as variation; and creativity as originality. These can be linked to Bloom's stages as follows:

TABLE 3.2 Fisher's facets of creativity vs Bloom's stages

creativity as generation	**clinamen** and **tessera**	the young writer generates writing in directly recreative tasks in response to the model – an imitation of 'voice'
creativity as variation	**kenosis** and **daemonisation**	the developing writer moves on, looking to vary and develop the 'voice' of the model
creativity as originality	**askesis** and **apophrades**	the mature writer masters his/her own 'voice' and is now able to return to the voice of the model and to use it as a tool, with originality

Bloom's observations conceptualise writerly development entirely through the writer's relationship with his/her reading. Like Kress, far from positing a straightforward relationship between the two, Bloom suggests that the process of assimilation and mastery of the craft of writing and the metamorphosis of reading into writing is demanding.

Creativity and originality

The search for a creative 'voice' and its relation to the issue of originality is problematic. Indeed, the better read a writer is, the more difficult may be the task of finding a 'voice'; the possibility for perceived originality becomes increasingly remote the more an individual has read, and as such the conceptualisation of creativity must be adjusted accordingly. Many pupils develop greater inhibitions about their abilities to write creatively the older they become, as a direct result of their widening frame of literary reference and their growing perceptions of their own inability to be original. Pupils need to be introduced to the idea that creativity is not necessarily synonymous with originality.

This is an issue that Bloom addresses significantly. His theory of the development of the writer's 'voice' depends upon the notion that creativity can only exist in response to previous writing and may not include traditional conceptualisations of 'originality' at all. T.S. Eliot casts further doubt on this issue when he suggests that:

No poet, no artist of any art, has his complete meaning alone. His significance, his appreciation is the appreciation of his relation to the dead poets and artists. You cannot value him alone; you must set him, for contrast and comparison, among the dead.[6]

The entire concept of originality is thus challenged. He goes on to relate this specifically to the creative processes of the poet:

The poet's mind is in fact a receptacle for seizing and storing up numberless feelings, phrases, images, which remain there until all the particles which can unite to form a new compound are present together.

The act of composition is thus seen as a process of accretion and alteration, the storing and reassembling of salient ideas, techniques, words and images until they coalesce to form a new creative work. This is a useful concept to apply to the ways in which pupils learn the art of writing. Creativity is seen not as an isolated event but as an on-going process. As such, it is susceptible to teaching and learning. By targeting teaching at component elements of creativity, such as the formation of images, the use of the senses, the development of metaphor and simile and the forms and conventions of a variety of genres, teachers can facilitate the development of creative awareness and creative skills in their pupils.

What is creative writing?

The concept of creativity and its development in creative writing is problematic. Indeed, the term 'creative writing' itself presents difficulties. Arguably, any act of writing can be seen as a 'creative' act. Even in transcription the writer engages in an act of recreation, taking control of organising, paragraphing and punctuating speech, recording inflection and the speakers' pose in order to 'create' a documentary record. The writer, to communicate successfully, must enter into an active and imaginary dialogue with the reader. The act of writing is by its very nature both creative and dramatic. The concept of creativity should not be limited therefore. A letter written to a friend or to an imaginary recipient requires no less the functions of creativity than the composition of a story. The production of a piece of persuasive writing requires just the same creative engagement with the 'audience' as does the writing of a poem.

The following letter provides an example of the role of creativity within a response by a Year 7 pupil; the task required the composition of a formal letter of complaint about the content of an episode of the television police drama *The Bill*:

Example of a first draft – what are the signs of creativity?

> Mr T.V. Programme
> B.B.C. T.V.
> London.

To Dear Mr tV programme,

I am write to complain about the vilonce I sore last night on last nights bill. Their were lots of times when I felt the need to turn over as lots of times I felt sickend. I am a great lover of the programme and look forward to watching it however, last night the programme portrayed the police in an unessassary light. I used to be a police man myself and the force that p.c. Quinnon was seen to use on that drug dealer was to explitic. Young people today have a very bad view of the police and this programme did not help there image. If my young granddaughter had seen the programme what would she had thought.

I hope you will note my complain and continue to make the bill in the fashion I have come acustome to.

While it contains a number of errors, this response demonstrates a number of important creative and imaginative characteristics:

- the views expressed provide evidence of an ability to express opinions clearly and appropriately, creatively engaging with a point of view;
- the pupil adopts a suitable register and tone to develop the reader's perception of the writer's 'voice', thus demonstrating the ability creatively to operate with language to build effect ('the programme portrayed the police in an unessassary light', 'continue to make the bill in the fashion I have come acustome to', 'I felt sickend');
- the pupil adopts a writerly 'persona' other than his own; this persona is developed by the provision of incidental detail ('I used to be a police man myself', 'my young granddaughter') to build the reader's impression of the ex-policeman grandfather;
- while rudimentary, the use of an address and the identification of an addressee demonstrate the writer's awareness of the purpose of this piece of writing and his abilities to create efficiently within the form required.

Selection and writing

In any act of writing, selection in three areas is essential. To produce an effective piece of writing, the writer must have a clearly defined sense of:

- content
- audience
- purpose.

The synthesis of these three elements constitutes the essential act of creativity in writing. Any written composition, regardless of its genre or intention, needs to establish an effective 'dialogue' between the writer and the reader. The burden of responsibility for the efficient operation of this dialogue, of course, lies with the writer – and it is precisely here that the writer needs to be most creative. Choices as to content, vocabulary, structure and reference will all define the extent to which the dramatic dialogue between the writer and the reader can operate. The writer needs critically to refine the relationship between the content, the audience and the purpose of the writing in order to create a text suitable for the reader. Such refinement can only occur effectively through a structured process of writing, which enables the writer to create a text suiting the needs of each of these elements.

It is essential that teachers introduce their pupils to a carefully structured process of writing and encourage them in the application of it, targeting each of these three aspects equally and ensuring pupils establish the key links between them.

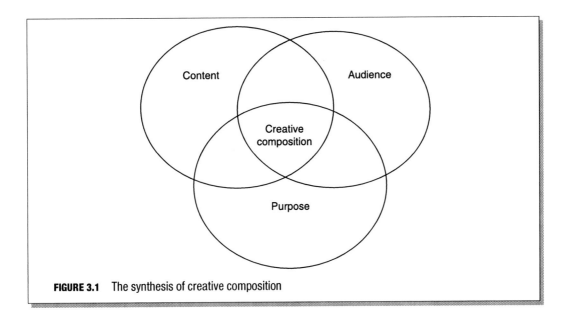

FIGURE 3.1 The synthesis of creative composition

Writing as process

One of the biggest dangers in the teaching of writing is that undue focus is placed on content at the expense of a detailed consideration of the creative process. Such a view encourages pupils and teachers alike to view writing as a product rather than as a mechanism; as a summative article of expression rather than as a formative tool in the development of thought.

The importance of writing as a creative mechanism of thought should never be underestimated. 'Fetch me a pen, I need to think,' Voltaire once famously quipped; and E.M. Forster, in one of the seminal works on fictional writing, commented: 'How can I know what I think until I see what I write'.[7] Behind both of these observations lies the essential recognition that writing is an integral part of creation and creativity, not the end product of it. Teachers and pupils – if effective writing is to take place, and if an atmosphere of true creativity is to be established – must recognise the process of writing as innately valuable.

The process of writing may be broken down into the following stages:

A process for writing

planning

↓

drafting

↓

editing

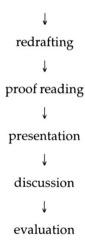

$\downarrow$

redrafting

$\downarrow$

proof reading

$\downarrow$

presentation

$\downarrow$

discussion

$\downarrow$

evaluation

This may seem a cumbersome and lengthy process and may vary according to the conditions under which a piece of writing is undertaken. Equally, the central sections of the process may be undertaken more than once as a piece of writing evolves through a series of developmental redraftings. This model provides a thorough, reflective and interactive approach to the act of writing. It sees writing not as a terminal outcome but as part of an ever-evolving process. The genesis, development, presentation and future impact of the writing are all brought to the fore, enabling pupils and teachers alike to engage in detail with the writing at every stage. Teaching at the point of composition, in order to develop and improve, becomes an essential component of the work of writing. This model also suggests the importance of corporate responses to pupil-written text.

Another sequence for writing (outlined in the table on page 47) is suggested by the National Strategy.[8] The right-hand column indicates the author's response to what each stage in this process suggests.

This model begins the process of writing at a different point. The integral link established in the early phases between the pupils' writing and teacher-provided exemplar materials is an essential basis for the preparatory work for the writing sequence. Exploratory reading and questions to prompt critical reflection can be used to introduce the pupils to the features, conventions and writerly tools ('how it is written') typical of a particular type of text. Here Gunther Kress's observation that 'neither the process of reading nor that of writing can be understood in isolation from the other'[9] becomes significant. The introduction of pupils to a range of 'model' texts is an essential part of their development into effective writers. These 'models' can then be applied through the provision of writing supports such as writing frames. These can vary widely, restricting or opening the task according to the needs of the pupil and the purpose of the writing exercise. Writing supports must be thoughtfully applied to target pupils' individual requirements and to allow them to explore and play with the possibilities of the creative tools they are learning within their own writing.

TABLE 3.3 Sequence for writing

1	Establish clear aims	Clarify writing objectives
2	Provide example(s)	Introduce writing models
3	Explore the features of the text	Look into generic features of models
4	Define the conventions	Explain typical language/content conventions of the genre
5	Demonstrate how it is written	Teacher writes, employing generic features and conventions explored above
6	Compose together	Shared writing
7	Scaffold the first attempts	Provision of differentiated writing frames or other writing support
8	Independent writing	Independent application of writerly tools and generic conventions learned
9	Draw out key learning	Return to key features for reinforcement of learning
10	Review	Formative evaluation of uses of learning

The use of scaffolding techniques to support the pupils in their initial attempts at composition offer the writer the opportunity to operate at an interim level as a stepping-stone on the way to independence. Care has to be taken with the use of such scaffolding devices, however, as two potential dangers threaten

- that pupils develop an undue dependence upon the provision of such frames, so that they cease to be an interim aid and become an essential support; and
- that pupils can be constrained by the limits of the frame and thus find their creative urges to explore tasks in individual ways stymied.

There follows an example of a writing frame which is deliberately restrictive:

Example: a restrictive writing frame

In this activity, Year 6 pupils were required to write a journalistic account of events in the run-up to Noah's Flood (diagram page 48).

There are advantages and disadvantages to this type of writing frame in the development of creativity. The outlining of the content and presentation of the writing response remains firmly under the control of the teacher. This allows for a tight focus on the structural, formal, linguistic and stylistic features of writing within the journalistic medium by removing any concerns with regard to the content and organisation of material: the requirement for creativity in terms of the 'what' of writing is reduced to tighten the focus on linguistic and stylistic creation within the prescribed parameters of the writing frame. This is clearly of benefit to young writers who need to develop

HEADLINE

SUB-HEADING

REPORTER'S NAME	PICTURE

INTRODUCTION

To include:

When
Where
Who
What was found by the reporter

MAIN BODY OF ARTICLE

By-line
Noah's viewpoint
Neighbours' viewpoint
Other organisations interested in events (e.g. RSPCA, local council)
Quotes
Noah's family's opinions
Eyewitness accounts
Spokesperson from the local church
Weather forecasters

CONCLUDING STATEMENT/SUMMING UP

skills within this area, or those who are effective story*tellers* but weaker story *writers*. Restriction of the writing task can provide positive benefits in terms of focus.

For stronger writers, however – those whom we may term 'talented' – such a frame may well prove restrictive in a pejorative sense. More secure in their grasp of the linguistic and stylistic requirements of the medium they may well wish to develop their ideas in a more fluid and less constrained way, breaking free from the prescribed content and format. This is not to suggest that writing frames have no place in the work of stronger writers – what is a genre of writing but a large-scale writing frame? – but rather to observe that a different and looser frame may prove beneficial. For such writers, techniques such as story-mapping may prove more effective tools, whereby the writer is required to develop a visual generic structure and plan for writing. Alternatively, the provision of an open stimulus, such as an object, a piece of music, a map, a photograph, a film or a picture, accompanied by a structured introduction to, and 'reading' of, the stimulus in an act of collaborative planning can pave the way to more open-framed writing tasks.

The picture reproduced as Figure 3.2 was provided to a class of Year 6 pupils as a stimulus to a piece of writing with the purpose of conveying emotion.

The class, collaboratively, in small groups and individually, considered the picture, focusing particularly on the girl's expression, her clothing, the background and her likely emotional state, developing, as they went, banks of vocabulary and devising a story map for their piece of writing. The only restrictions, aside from the purpose of the writing, were in terms of historical 'time' and location. Extracts from two examples of the work resulting are reproduced below.

Example of writing derived from picture

I had just finished painting the hills, fields and sheep when this girl about twenty-five years old came running towards me. She sat down on a rock in front of me and asked if I could paint her. She was Irish like me, I could tell by her accent. She could have run away from home, as many Irish immigrants had nowhere to go and no houses to live in. I had come here because of terrors in my hometown in Ireland.

As I started to sketch I saw a sadness in her eyes. This was understandable because coming from Ireland to Britain myself I know the things it puts you through. Trauma, depression and isolation – these are the things I felt and I started to wonder. There were a couple of possibilities. One: she could have left her family behind in Ireland, or Two: something had happened, for example, a tragedy.

As I thought these thoughts, I felt an anxiety to run away from this place and get on the next boat back to Ireland. But I knew I couldn't. As I neared the end of my painting I glimpsed a man out of the corner of my eye, walking across the fields holding an oil lamp. The girl I was painting turned her head towards him . . .

The light was bright and as the man came nearer the light shone bright in my eyes. The sky was darkening and I put my hand up to shield my eyes. The man called out a name – I thought it was Patricia, but as the wind was picking up I couldn't tell for sure. I was distracted by all of this and had totally forgotten about the painting and when I finally turned my head, the painting was gone and the man and the girl made off with the painting. I packed up with a sigh and started making my way towards my house at the bottom of the hill.

When I woke at dawn I was rested and after I had eaten I started to wonder where they had gone with the portrait. It was market day and I needed some paints and food. As I made my way towards the market square I thought about the night before and the girl's face in my mind. I reached the town and brought my things home and got ready to set up my painting utensils. As I walked into the field I saw that the rock the maiden sat on yesterday was occupied again. I was

FIGURE 3.2 Picture stimulus: *Evening Thoughts* by Robert Herdman (National Gallery of Scotland)

amazed. When I got to the rock I saw the portrait of her I had done yesterday. As I sat down I saw she was crying. Her face was an island with streams crossing and intercrossing all over and eventually they ran into the sea at her feet. Her mouth was an arch leading to a place full of sorrow and her eyes were a vortex trailing away to a distant place. She was a complete picture of total misery along with her life I thought suddenly. Eventually after a long five minutes she handed me my painting. Afterwards she sat in total silence watching me paint, sketch and draw. When the sun started lowering in the west, the clouds covered and again, the same as yesterday, I noticed the man with the light making his way across the moor.

This writer has clearly flourished within the freedom allowed by this type of writing frame, producing a composition containing evidence of sophistication and narrative flair:

- there is an almost metafictional 'discovery' in the use of the painter, as the writer undergoes a process of discovery in the writing – this demonstrates the writer's sophisticated sense of narrative technique;
- the writer confidently uses varied sentences and ellipses for emotional and narrative impact;
- there is an imaginative use of the persona of the painter to create the reader's view of the girl; the emotional states of both characters are explored;
- incidental use of detail from the picture – sheep, sky, rock – adds colour to the writing, functioning integrally within the overall impact of the piece;
- development of the context of Irish immigration provides a rationale for the girl's emotions and the painter's emotional response to her;
- striking use is made of metaphor in the concluding paragraph;
- suspense and uncertainty are created in the final paragraph as to whether we are looking at the portrait or the girl herself; and
- the possible conflation of the artist and the nameless man in the final paragraph hints at further possibilities of narrative depth.

Another example

She always came to the rock whenever she was depressed or sad. Her family were trading illegal tabaco for huge areas of land. She only found out a few days ago. She was so confused, bewilderd. She was seeing a man David Smith that her father had forbid her to see. So she did not want her father to find out because she was afraid he might beat her. She had to tell someone, just to get it off her chest. She could tell her boyfriend but she would have to trust him with the burden. Her love for him was so strong, she could trust him with any thing. She decided to tell him, she told him to meet her at the rock. A figure appeard on the hill and started to approach, but was it him?

This pupil is far less well served by the looser writing frame:

- the writing remains largely at the level of a simple narrative;

- the narrative provides background to the girl's emotional state, but does not creatively engage in building a fuller appreciation of these emotions;

- use of detail from stimulus – the rock, the land, the hill – is limited in impact; and

- the lack of concrete guidance with regard to content and structure has left this pupil, who would be better served by a more restrictive writing frame (see above), struggling to engage with the creative task demanded.

Shared writing and the creative process

Particular emphasis is placed, within the National Strategy, upon the technique of Shared Writing, an activity during which teachers and pupils collaborate in the creation of a shared text. Initially, the teacher writes while 'thinking aloud', linking language and content choices to the purpose of the writing and the needs of the audience. The pupils are then drawn into the process, and are likewise required to 'think aloud' as they share continued composition together, making transparent the thought processes lying behind their authorial decisions and discussing the impact of these decisions upon the reader. Such a corporate approach to writing has both its benefits and its drawbacks. While the verbally confident, in both written and oral modes, will be likely to contribute, those who are less confident in these areas – even where a supportive and mutually respectful classroom environment has been established – will be much less likely to offer their responses. The opportunity for such pupils to benefit from a detailed commentary on the writing processes involved in composition and to begin to evaluate the writing in critical terms, however, is clearly to be desired. Additional difficulties can arise where differences of opinion over content, vocabulary and stylistic choices emerge, although this can lead to fruitful discussions of the alternative materials under consideration if carefully and sensitively handled by the teacher.

Conclusion

The key to success in teaching creative writing is to teach pupils to enter into a critical engagement with their own writing. The two processes for writing considered in this chapter need to operate side by side in the development of independent, fully creative writers. Both models end with a recognition of the importance of review and evaluation, whether by the teacher, by the group, by peers or by the individual. This highlights the importance of formative assessment techniques in the on-going creative teaching of writing. Pupils must, with the help of their teachers, become involved in the active review of their own work so that they become aware of the importance of the transference of skills between writing tasks and see their development as writers in sequential rather than in unitary terms.

The value inherent in each of these models is the focus on the 'how' of writing rather than merely on the 'what'. This makes for an interactive and developing sense of writing as an evolving skill. Teachers need to be encouraged into teaching at the point of writing, seeking ways in which to engage pupils in critical reflection on their composition and prompting them to explore the processes in which they have been involved.

Writing is about taking risks with words and structures. In the truly creative classroom pupils and teachers alike will push at the boundaries of a class's and the individual's achievement. While structured and focused teaching is clearly essential in the development of pupil literacy and in their growth as effective and creative writers, the imposition of too rigid a framework is ultimately stultifying. In a system increasingly driven by the needs and demands of assessment, it would be all too easy for the teaching of writing to be reduced to teaching by correction after the event, where engagement is a reactive response rather than a proactive force. If we as teachers wish our pupils to take flight as writers we must be involving them in a creative and exciting process of calculated risk – a safe process in which they are free to explore and to extend the bounds of their own originality.

Therefore, let the final word go to Thomas Edison: 'Hell, there are no rules – we're trying to accomplish something'.

Notes

1   Larkin, P. *Collected Poems*, Faber, 2001.

2   In *Better Writers* (Courseware Publications, 2001) Debra Myhill explores a range of practical approaches to children's writing.

3   'Interrelations of reading and writing' by G.Kress, in *The Writing of Writing* (ed. Andrew Wilkinson), Open University Press, 1986, presents a stimulating account of the cross-fertilisation of reading and writing as processes, exploring the complex but essential link between the two.

4   *Key Stage 3 National Strategy Improving Writing*, DfES, 2003.

5   Harold Bloom's *The Anxiety of Influence: A Theory of Poetry*, Oxford University Press, 1973, looks in detail at the issues of poetic inspiration in creative compositional processes, re-evaluating the place of originality in writing.

6   In 'Tradition and the individual talent', *The Sacred Wood*, 1922, T.S.Eliot reflects in detail on his own creative processes and argues strongly for the need for poets to create within the tradition of poetry. He significantly questions the extent to which any author can or should be totally original.

7   E.M. Forster's classic, *Aspects of the Novel*, 1927, offers an interesting insight into the elements and processes of fictional composition.

8   Key Stage 3 National Strategy, *English Department Training 2001: Writing Non-fiction*, DfES.

9   Kress, G. 'Interrelations of reading and writing', in *The Writing of Writing* (ed. Andrew Wilkinson), Open University Press, 1986.

Further reading

Bloom, H. (1973) *The Anxiety of Influence: A Theory of Poetry*. Oxford University Press.

Coleridge,T.S. (1999) *Kubla Khan*. Penguin.

DfES (2001) *English Department Training 2001: Writing Non-fiction* Key Stage 3 National Strategy.

DfES (2003) *Improving Writing*. Key Stage 3 National Strategy.

Dickens, C. (2003), *Nicholas Nickelby*. Penguin.

Dickens, C. (2003), *Oliver Twist*. Penguin.

Eliot, T.S. (1997) 'Tradition and the individual talent', in *The Sacred Wood*. Faber & Faber.

Forster, E.M. (1976) *Aspects of the Novel*. Penguin.

Joyce, J. (2002) *Finnegan's Wake*. Faber & Faber.

Kerouac, J. (2000) *On the Road*. Penguin Modern Classics.

Kress, G. (1986) 'Interrelations of reading and writing', in Wilkinson, A. (ed.) *The Writing of Writing*. Open University Press.

Larkin, P. (2001) *Collected Poems*. Faber & Faber.

Martin, N. (1983) *Mostly About Writing*, London: Heinemann

Martin, N. *et al.* (1976) *Writing and Learning across the Curriculum 11–16*. Schools Council Publications.

Myhill, D. (1999) 'Writing matters'. *English in Education*, 33(3), 70–81.

Myhill, D. (2001) *Better Writers*. Courseware Publications.

Myhill, D. (2001), 'Why shaping and crafting'. *English in Education*, 5(1), 15–19.

Myhill, D. (2001) Writing: creating and crafting'. *English in Education*, 35(3), 13–20.

Protherough, R. (1983) *Encouraging Writing*: Methuen.

Shelley, M. (2003) *Frankenstein, or The Modern Prometheus*. Penguin.

Wilkinson, A. (ed.) (1986) *The Writing of Writing*. Open University Press.

Creative drama: thinking from within

Colleen Johnson

'Drama is such a normal thing . . . All it demands is that children think from within a dilemma, instead of talking about a dilemma.'

(Dorothy Heathcote (quoted in 1995))

TO BECOME EFFECTIVE LEARNERS children need access to activities through which they may gain deeper understanding of their own creative processes. Drama provides a limitless range of contexts, rich with opportunities for developing such understanding. The subject demands 'actively thinking from within a situation', and with reflection at the core of good drama practice children have the chance to explore and develop their own thinking. This chapter explores ways in which teachers have used drama to enhance creative thinking, both individually and collaboratively, with critical reflection being at the heart of the process. It makes a case for the increased status of drama in schools and in teacher training through a consideration of:

- the arts and thinking skills;
- drama and creative thinking;
- strategies for the classroom;
- teacher questioning; and
- process to performance.

The arts and thinking skills

Recent initiatives, both nationally and internationally, have focused on the development of thinking skills in arts education (NFER 2000). For example, in the wake of CASE (Cognitive Acceleration through Science Education)[1], which sought to promote higher-level thinking in pupils through Science activities, the Arts Reasoning and Thinking Skills Project was launched in the north-east of England. The project aims to 'raise standards of attainment both within Arts subjects and across the whole curriculum'.[2] In Australia, students training to teach in secondary schools are being encouraged to use drama strategies in their teaching 'whatever their subject, to get to know their students better, in order to teach them more effectively through helping them develop their thinking skills'.[3] Of course, no-one would want to argue that the role of art, dance, drama and music is simply to serve learning across other areas of the curriculum. This would be to seriously underestimate the importance of the arts as subjects in their own right. However, if advocates for drama can show how the subject may be used to enhance learning, and thinking, generally, then we have a convincing argument for its higher status in the curriculum.

Drama and creative thinking

Children are active thinkers and learn in verbal, visual and kinaesthetic ways and 'possibly drama more than any other art form, combines the verbal, visual and kinaesthetic for the learner'.[4] We need to consider in more detail the types of thinking which drama demands of its participants. McGuinness (1999) has analysed what she perceives as elements of 'high quality thinking' and Baldwin (2002) identifies links between these and high-quality drama. Three of these aspects will be focused upon and related to classroom practice in the discussion that follows.

High-quality thinking:

- is complex, requiring consideration of several viewpoints;
- can involve the application of multiple criteria, which may sometimes be at odds with one another; and
- incorporates making and imposing meaning.

High-quality drama affords the active experience of the same situation from different standpoints; for example, through role play various perspectives of those people involved in a particular situation can be explored. Drama also affords the opportunity for creative approaches to the resolution of dilemma and conflict, both in and out of role. High-quality drama is characterised by finding and sharing meaning and understanding and then conveying this shared understanding to others as audience.

In the two examples from practice which follow, the generic aims were to:

- use drama to think creatively and critically;
- create opportunities for the children to reflect on their thinking, and possibly shift their thinking, both in and out of role.

In good drama practice, children usually play adults or children at least three years older than their real selves. This requires them to strive to find the language appropriate to the role and situation. Such activities place immense demands upon children's thinking and language.

Strategies for the classroom

Example 4.1 – Year 5: 'The Way West'

The drama theme chosen was taken from *Drama Structures* (O'Neill and Lambert 1982). Although this text was written for use with children in Key Stage 3, many of the schemes of work can be used very effectively in Key Stage 2 with little or no adaptation. This illustrates the point that the processes of drama are largely transferable between different ages and key stages. The levels of sophistication of work will be dictated by the maturity of the group and by the teacher's skill in guiding and challenging thinking. The dramatic stimulus can be the same for all.

Entitled 'The Way West', the topic is based upon the movement of settlers across America in the mid-1800s, and offers scope for exploring situations in which people are forced to make difficult decisions as they strive for a better life. The teacher began by showing the children a copy of a black-and-white photograph of a group of American 'pioneers' – two families, taken in the mid-nineteenth century and asked them what the photograph suggested to them.

The children deduced that these were poor people, possibly resting during a long journey. Although the teacher gave a few historical facts, it was surprising how much they were able to add, 'building on experiences and knowledge of others in the group' (O'Neill and Lambert ibid.) collectively. By the end of this brief introduction they had decided that the photograph was taken over a hundred years ago and that these were people travelling, in America, from the Mid West to the Oregon, a hazardous journey of over two thousand miles. The image led to the first drama strategy used.

Teacher and children in role

The teacher introduced the activity by saying that 'all of us will be acting together' with the children taking on the roles of members of a small Mid-West town community. They were meeting in the village hall because they had been told that 'a government representative was coming to talk to them'. In the role of the representative she presented them with the opportunity for a 'better life' by offering them the chance of moving to the state of Oregon, painting an attractive picture of a pleasant climate, free farming land and prosperity for 'any of the pioneering spirits who wanted to better their lives'. After some discussion and questions she asked for a show of hands to indicate numbers likely to make the journey. Almost all hands were raised, enthusiastically. She then instructed them to 'go home and talk through the idea with their families'. She would return later to see who had decided to go.

Improvisation

The children, working in groups as families, then discussed the proposal. Suddenly initial responses were challenged. As the families talked through and considered arguments both for and against the journey, doubts emerged. A number of conflicting opinions were articulated. Standpoints needed to be justified. Here was complex thinking brought about through the active engagement in assessing a situation from different standpoints.

Following these improvisations, the teacher in role asked for a show of hands to indicate the level of willingness to undertake the journey now and remarked on a significant drop in number! She asked the question: Why are you now less keen on going on the journey to the Oregon? The following responses were given:

'It's hard leaving your home.'
'My father is too old to go so we will have to leave him behind.'
'I think it might be dangerous.'
'I don't know anybody who has been.'

Here were elements of reflection in role and an explicit awareness of how the children's thinking had changed through both collective and individual reflection during and beyond the dramatic experience that illustrates the point that 'thinking from within a situation immediately forces a different kind of thinking'(O'Neill 1995) – a creative response to the situation.

The teacher asked the children, out of role, to hypothesise about possible motives the government may have had for encouraging the move. Suggestions included:

'They feel sorry for us.'
'They want to have our land.'
'They want more people to fight the Indians.'

During the discussion, one child said, 'What if it's all lies?' In fact, in the mid-1800s the ownership of the Oregon territory was being disputed by the United States and Great Britain. The US government was hoping to capitalise on establishing right of occupation, thanks to the migration into the state of large numbers of people. The children were right to be suspicious!

In subsequent drama sessions, as they became familiar with the plight of the travellers, the children developed a growing empathy with them. The teacher asked the children if any part of the drama had reminded them of a time in their own lives, or any current events. They were invited to share their thoughts with the rest of the class. Responses included moving house, saying goodbye to a grandparent going home to India, and coming home from holidays and leaving behind friends. Other connections were made with the war in Palestine and the familiar television news images of families being displaced.

Drama provides a vehicle for children to put into words their own emotional response to events, which they may never have discussed before. It invites thinking at a deeper and more creative level. The journals completed as part of the activity provided evidence of continued reflection (see below), which stimulated empathetic writing:

At first I thought Wow! a better life for my dad, sister and daughters, but she never told us anything bad about the Oregon. It sounds too good.

That woman smiled a lot and made it sound good but now I don't know what to think. I feel like they are playing tricks on us. When people want something from you they always smile.

It makes me think of my Great Granny who was 97 and died last year. She was too old to go anywhere. If this had been then, I don't think we would leave her behind.

When I saw the picture of them I thought they are brave to go on the journey because of snakes and the mountains. But when I was the dad (in the improvisation) I think you have to be brave to make decisions because if it goes wrong your family blames you.

Furthermore, Martha said, 'Drama makes you think about what's going on around you.' To this, the teacher asked,' How?' Martha answered, 'Because you do things in drama but some people do those things in life and you know how it feels'. Martha is articulating the empathy (creative understanding of others) which engaging in drama facilitates. If we are to maintain a holistic approach to education we must value all learning, including that which could be termed as spiritual, social and moral. 'We must not neglect learning about what it means to be human' (Baldwin 2002) and drama 'provides a vehicle for exploring human experience' (Neelands 1992), fostering empathy for the human condition, creating opportunities for those involved to actively imagine what it is like to be someone else. This experience, according to writer Ian McKewan, speaking just after 11 September 2001, 'is at the core of humanity. It is the essence of compassion and is the beginning of humanity' (McKewan 2001).

Still image

This strategy requires children to organise themselves into creating a three-dimensional image to represent a dramatic moment or a visual 'summing up' of a situation. Children are already familiar with the convention of the still image under many guises: for example, a pause on a video is a 'freeze frame', or they may have played 'musical statues', or sequenced a story using cartoon strips and added captions to 'snapshots' (Johnson 2000). For the teacher with little or no experience of drama, this is an invaluable technique, offering a means of controlling a dramatic situation.

In groups, in role as the travellers, the children were asked to show a significant incident on their journey, to represent the attendant perils and hardships and the effects such experiences had upon them. They were then asked to represent these in still images, one after another.

The approach, once modelled by the teacher with the whole class, is useful for children to use for themselves, independently of the teacher. For example, children in groups can be asked to choose the most significant part of an improvisation they have just completed, and then to create a still image to represent this, to show to the rest of the class. This involves highly focused discussion as the children negotiate meaning and how to convey their interpretation to an audience. It is more fruitful and less time consuming, to have an image to develop rather than a short improvisation, as children merely have to select a significant moment in the narrative. The image created by the group will represent two things: a key moment or event and the quality of learning achievable through exploratory talk. The *still image* is a powerful strategy which children quickly learn to manage without the aid of the teacher, therefore encouraging a level of independence. Such work illustrates the link between high-quality thinking which involves creatively seeking to make meaning through a shared understanding, and then to convey this meaning through performance.

As the teacher and children looked at each image, she invited observers to comment on what they were seeing: What did they think the image represented? What was the mood of those involved? Could they predict the outcome of the events portrayed? If they could ask questions of any of those characters in the image, what would they be? How had the image deepened knowledge and understanding of the travellers and their plight? In the group's attempt to convey meaning to us, what worked well and why? This last question is crucial to such work, inviting critical and positive reflection to enhance self-esteem and to encourage children's creative learning in drama.

Thought tracking

Using this strategy the teacher invites those in the still image to contribute the thoughts by speaking them aloud – of the characters they are representing, one at a time. This encourages children to clarify and rationalise their thinking. For example, at one stage in the story, the children were divided into two groups: one representing the travellers at a point where they were about to enter 'tribal land', which they would need to cross in order to continue their journey. The other group were in role as the tribe who had been warned that strangers were approaching. Following discussion in role, key questions emerged, such as: 'How will the two groups communicate if they do not share the same language?'

Reflection

Collective and individual reflection is critical if children are to discover and articulate what the experience means, or has meant, to them. For 'experience itself is neither productive nor unproductive; it is how you reflect on it that makes it significant' (Heathcote and Bolton 1995 : 164).

Time was allotted for children's discussion both during and following the lessons. In addition, the teacher produced reflective journals for the children to keep throughout the four weeks and beyond. In these the children were required to reflect on their thinking both during and after the dramatic experience. The quality of empathetic writing that such work produced shows children were continuing to reflect on their experience between and beyond the drama lessons.

Teacher questioning

Drama offers scope for a wide range of questions both in and out of role, and those posed to encourage reflection demand deep thinking on the part of the children. Key questions were used at points throughout the lessons as well as in the reflective journal, pushing children to justify their opinions, speculations and hypotheses. In addition to the range of questions generated by the still images (above), were the following:

Questions in role

Why are you now less keen on going on the journey to the Oregon?
How did it feel to say goodbye to friends and family?
Were you confident you had made the right decision? Why?
Were there points on the journey when you had doubts?
Did you blame anyone for what happened?
How did you feel when you first saw the 'promised land' of Oregon?
What do people need to build a community?
How will you resolve differences in the community?
What do you need to protect yourselves from?
How has this experience changed you?
What lies ahead for these pioneer people? What makes you think that?

Questions out of role

In our drama today, what worked well and why?
What did you enjoy about our drama today? Why?
What made you feel uncomfortable? Why?
Is there anyone in the class whose performance you have enjoyed today? Why?
Do you think that those who chose to go made a good decision? Why?
Was it morally right? Why? If not, why not?
What does this moment in drama make you think of? Why?
Has your thinking changed about any aspect of this story? Why?

Fisher acknowledges the need for 'a period of gestation to allow for . . . "soft thinking" to take place' (see Chapter 1), and this is important in relation to engagement in drama. The teacher gave opportunities for the children to reflect longitudinally on the drama process, both through discussion and through reflective writing in the journals. As with children, when adults see a film, a television drama or a play in the theatre they too may think about it for several days, months or even years. The initial dramatic 'stimulus' is of the moment, but our thinking can be influenced by the experience for a long time. We enjoy the opportunity to share our reflections with others, just as children do. This offers further opportunity for creative, critical, reflective thinking.

Example 4. 2 – *Where the Wild Things Are*

A Year 2 class had been reading *Where the Wild Things Are* by Maurice Sendak. It is the story of Max, a boy, sent to bed 'without any supper' as a punishment for his mischievous behaviour. Suddenly, from his room he embarks upon a journey to a different land where he encounters the 'wild things' – huge and, initially, scary monsters. Eventually he becomes their 'king' but finally leaves them to return home. At last he arrives safely back 'into the night of his very own room', where, it appears, time has stood still. The teacher used a number of drama strategies, partly to help meet Literacy Strategy Objectives (DfEE 1999b) but also to mine the story for potential issues and dilemmas in order to foster creative thinking, working both within the text and beyond the traditional ending to the story.

Still image/thought tracking

The teacher said, 'We are going to re-enact the moment when Max saw the wild things for the very first time'. She divided the class in two, those in one half to play 'Max' and the others to play the wild things. She asked those in this second group to choose one of the monsters (depicted by Sendak in glorious illustrations). She then said, 'find a space and make yourself into the wild thing you have chosen to be. On the first signal (the shaking of a tambourine) you can move around but on the second signal you must freeze.' The children spent a few minutes walking around, getting into character, exaggerating their steps to represent the large, ungainly creatures walking. She shook the tambourine for the second time. The children 'froze' into grotesque images! She narrated:

> And when he came to the place where the wild things are they roared their terrible roars and gnashed their terrible teeth and rolled their terrible eyes and showed their terrible claws.

She then invited the first group, as Max, to wander around and between all the still images of the wild things. She moved between them, inviting each Max to speak her or his thoughts aloud, prompting them with 'At this moment I am thinking to myself . . .'. The children, as Max, responded:

'I'm terrified'
'Oh no, monsters!'
'They'll kill me with their spiky teeth.'
'I want to go home!'
'How did I get here?'
'Is this a nightmare?'
'They are so big.'

After a few moments she asked the children, in role as Max, to freeze too. Then she said, 'Remember your positions and facial expressions'. She 'unfroze' the children in one half of the room so that they could look at the images of Max and the wild things created by those in the other half. Then she swapped them over so that all were able to see each other's representations of the dramatic encounter. In each case she gave opportunities for the children to describe the expressions they saw, on both the monsters' as well as the Max's faces, and to speculate what Max might decide to do next. Even though most stories written for young children have a happy ending, when working, and thinking, as characters within the story, they cannot know what the future holds for them, hence experiencing 'the unpredictable', so crucial to creative thinking as discussed in Chapter 1.

Out of role, the teacher asked the children to think about a time when they had been frightened, like Max, and to describe what they remembered of their thinking at that moment. Tara said: 'When I saw a spider crawling out of my shoe just before I put it on . . . I jumped out of my skin'. The teacher asked, 'Why?', and Tara replied, 'Because I thought it would come and get me'.

James replied, 'I saw the big dinosaurs at the museum and they started moving. I was very scared. I wanted to run away'. (These were part of the automated display at the Natural History Museum in London.) There was laughter from the other children, alongside hums and nods of agreement. Through careful questioning the teacher enabled the children to explore together the ways in which they had coped with their fears, both rational and irrational.

Tara: I know spiders are only small so it wouldn't hurt me but when you are scared you think things are bigger.

Hardeep: You have to remember the spider is more scared of you because you could squash him.

James: My Mum stood right next to the dinosaur and it didn't eat her and I knew it wasn't real. But I was still scared.

Teacher and children in role

In a later session, based on what happened after Max had left the land of the wild things to return home, the teacher said, 'Now in our drama we are all going to play the wild thing'. She gave them time to get into role. She said, 'Gather round me, wild things. I have something to say'. They sat around her. She went on: 'As you know, it is about a week since Max left us to go back to his home. I miss Max; do you?' There was nodding in agreement. She asked, 'How are you all feeling now he's been gone for a few days?'

Gemma: I'm sad because Max has gone.

Nabil: I wish he'd come back.

Kamalpreet: It's boring now.

She went on, 'What do you miss most about him?' The children volunteered suggestions such as, 'He made me laugh', 'He was kind to me' and 'I liked him because he was different to us'. The teacher probed, 'How was he different?' Several children commented on his size or his clothes. Nancy said, 'I've never seen pyjamas before. Humans wear different clothes to go to sleep but we don't'. Nabil said, 'He did things differently. I think he thinks differently'. The teacher extended both his and the other children's thinking by asking, 'How do you know he thinks differently to you?' And so the discussion went on.

She then asked the children to find a partner. Each pair was to 'remember' a moment which Max and one of the wild things had shared and which might illustrate the qualities Max possessed. Subsequently, some of the short scenes were shown to others. These included Max sharing his sweets with a wild thing, teaching a wild thing to jump high, and so on. Following discussion, out of role, about what these examples had done to further knowledge of both Max and the wild things, she asked the children to go back into role as the latter. She continued, 'Wild things, it is clear that we all miss our friend so I have an idea. Let's go and visit him'. The initial response was enthusiastic and on two levels: *in role* the wild things were excited about the prospect of seeing Max again, and visiting a new land, where creatures like Max lived; *out of role* the children were excited about the dramatic journey they were about to share with their teacher. This led to the next strategy.

Mantle of the expert

The teacher asked, 'How can we get to where Max lives? I've never left this land before.' Various suggestions were made, mainly focusing on a boat journey because, after all, Max had arrived on a boat. She raised the problem, 'We don't have a boat. What can we do?' Several of the children suggested that they all make a boat. She replied, 'Well, I have seen a boat – the one Max came in – but I have no idea how to make one. Can you think of what we should do first?' The 'wild things' pooled their ideas, their knowledge and expertise. A list was written, with the teacher scribing, and then followed much activity while the boat was built.

Here the children took on the role of *experts* with knowledge and experience greater than those of the teacher in role. When children wear the mantle of the expert, the roles of teacher and pupils are temporarily reversed. The children are the 'ones in the know', who have the expertise and understanding to apply to the task in hand – in this case, deciding how to reach Max and how to build, and then steer, a boat, while the teacher in role is the 'one who needs to know', seeking their help and instruction (Johnson 2000).

Once the boat was ready and initial suggestions had been offered for how it was to be powered and so on, the teacher paused the drama and asked the children to reflect on the learning, which had just taken place. She drew attention to the language they had used in deciding how to build the boat and instructing each other on the building, and then the ways in which they might navigate. She asked, 'In our drama, what worked well and why?' The children were able to identify that the wild things had worked together to build the boat and had been able to make a plan for the journey. The teacher asked them, 'How do you know so much about boat building and sailing?' With the teacher's guidance the children were able to identify that all of them knew something about boats and that together they had 'pooled' their knowledge and understanding because the role and context had demanded it.

Next, she asked the children to 'find a space' as all would be in the role of Max. It was the moment when he saw the wild things arriving on their boat. *Still images* were created. Through *thought tracking*, a range of emotions was articulated:

'Oh, no! What will my Mum say?'
'They won't all fit in my house.'
'What if people make fun of them?'
'I am very happy they've come. I will take them to my school and if somebody picks on me they will fight them.'

The teacher asked the children to contrast Max's feelings at this point with those he had experienced when he had first seen the creatures on their own territory. The children identified that Max's fears were different now.

Improvisation

The children were again asked to work in pairs, one child represented Max and the other his mother. Max had to ask if his 'friends' could stay for a while, and to prepare her for meeting the wild things for the first time. It requires a considerable amount of creative imagination for a child to project her or himself into the role of a parent, responding to the careful guidance of another child in the role as his or her son, preparing to meet a monster! Again, the child, even working as Max – another child – is having to work hard to find the appropriate language to negotiate with a parent at such a critical moment.

Hot-seating

Toward the end of their stay with Max, some of the wild things were hot-seated. They were asked about their impressions of Max's world, and the differences between his and their own. This allowed the children to consider their own world (i.e. Max's) as it might be viewed by others. Stepping outside ourselves to view what is hitherto humdrum or 'normal' is an excellent way of reflecting upon, and even questioning, the rituals and customs we take for granted.

Process to performance

An element of performance is an integral part of process drama in that there is always a sense of audience among those creating the drama. However, occasionally it is possible to adapt work in order to create a performance for an audience beyond the classroom, using the children's discussion and selection of significant moments to write a script that communicates their response and understanding to others, and this necessitates a further metacognitive journey. This reflection is enhanced, as with the still image strategy, with the teacher's prompting question: 'What worked well and why?' The children then become used to and adept at reflecting upon the key dramatic moments which they have observed and shared. Being familiar with a range of drama tools, e.g. still image, helps them to select and refine them with a particular audience in mind. Such work makes demands upon children as armchair critics, offering them the opportunity to consider their own responses to performances and the performances of others they see within and beyond school.

A reflective journal can provide a focus for this process: with older children, this would be in their own writing but with younger children, a journal could be kept for the whole class and, during discussions following drama, key statements could be entered either by the teacher or a child, on behalf of those who had offered them. This provides written evidence of the children's continuing critical reflection, and growth in confidence in using of reflective language; a highly desirable, creative and transferable skill.

Conclusion

If 'thinking skills' can add value to learning, it is incumbent upon those of us engaged in arts education to make explicit what we have known for some time: that drama offers great potential for fostering the development of children's creative and critical thinking, and therefore drama merits a high status in primary education. Fisher acknowledges that 'the processes of creativity are not solely expressed through the arts' (Chapter 1). But if they are to found anywhere in primary education, it should surely be within high-quality arts teaching. This strengthens the argument for the inclusion of drama within whole-school curriculum planning, and its use as a mode of creative expression across all subjects.

We should rejoice in drama's welcome return to the primary curriculum both to support literacy and cross-curricular learning and to enable children to think and act more creatively. As Cecily O'Neill says, 'I like to see Drama as the cockroach in the curriculum. Just when you think it's been stamped out forever, it comes crawling back'.

Notes

1   The Cognitive Acceleration through Science Education programme (CASE) was pioneered by the Centre for the Advancement of Thinking at King's College, London (Adey and Shayer 1994).

2   Wigan Arts Project Writing Group, 2002.

3   Susan Wilks gave the keynote address at the Arts Reasoning and Thinking Skills Project Day in Wigan, 19 April 2002.

4   Patrice Baldwin gave the keynote address, entitled *Thinking Children* at the National Drama Conference in Edinburgh, April 2002.

Further reading

Adey, P. and Shayer, M. (1994) *Really Raising Standards*. London: Routledge.

Combes, A (1999) 'I'm glad you asked that: teacher questioning', in *The Times Educational Supplement* (22/01/1999).

DfEE (1998) *The National Literacy Strategy: Framework for Teaching*. London: HMSO.

DfEE (1999a) *English in the National Curriculum*. London: HMSO.

DfEE (1999b) *Opportunities for Drama in the Framework of Objectives*. London: HMSO.

Heathcote, D. (1965), in Drain, R. *Twentieth Century Theatre: A Sourcebook*. London: Routledge.

Heathcote, D. and Bolton, G. (1995) *Drama for Learning: An Account of Dorothy Heathcote's Mantle of the Expert Approach to Education*. Portsmouth, NH: Heinemann.

Hertrich, J. (1998) 'Drama', in OfSTED *Good Teaching in Art, Dance, Drama & Music*. London: Heinemann.

Johnson, C. (2000) 'What did I say?: speaking, listening and drama', in Fisher, R. and Williams, M. (eds) *Unlocking Literacy*. London: David Fulton.

Johnson, C. (2002) 'Drama and writing', in Williams, M. (ed.) *Unlocking Writing*. London: David Fulton.

McGuinness, C. (1999) *From Thinking Skills to Thinking Classrooms: A review and evaluation of approaches for developing pupils' thinking*. Norwich: HMSO.

McKewan, I. (2001), in *The Observer* (16/9/2001).

Neelands, J. (1992) *Learning through Imagined Experience*. London: Hodder & Stoughton.

NFER (2000) *Arts Education in Secondary Schools: Effects and Effectiveness*. Slough: NFER Publications Unit.

O'Neill C. and Lambert, A. (1982) *Drama Structures*. London: Hutchinson.

O'Neill, C. (1995) *Dramaworlds*. London: Heinemann.

Sendak, M. (1997) *Where the Wild Things Are*. London: Puffin.

Wilks, S. (1999), 'Improving critical thinking: the aesthetics and arts criticism strand of the Victorian CSF'. ART*cle*, Autumn/Winter.

Creative mathematics: allowing caged birds to fly

Debbie Robinson and Valsa Koshy

'Caged birds do sing, but what would be their song if they are sometimes allowed to fly'

(Ron Casey (1999))

'Once upon a time in the Land of Maths . . .'

(Shivani, aged 10)

Introduction

IN A TIGHTLY PACKED curriculum there may seem to be little space to squeeze in opportunities for children to be creative in mathematics. Teachers are under considerable pressure to gain approval by their children's progression along a speedy and rather linear journey through levels of achievement. In providing broader and more divergent experiences for the children they teach, teachers may be tempted to compromise success measured through results in national tests. To make time for creativity in mathematics education, teachers need to review what is taught and most significantly how it is taught. Indeed, they must question judgements about what really constitutes success in mathematics education. This chapter sets out to define creativity as an essential and central part of the mathematics curriculum. It offers practical suggestions to enable teachers to cultivate creativity in the teaching and learning of mathematics.

A national drive for creativity

In recent years there has been a national drive to encourage creativity in all aspects of education. In 1999 the National Advisory Committee on Creative and Cultural Education (NACCCE) made recommendations on the creative development of young people. Two further sources of support for a creative curriculum came from the Creativity project initiated by the Qualifications and Curriculum Authority, and more recently the Department for Education and Skills has made a strong commitment to developing the creative abilities of our children in a document entitled 'Excellence and Enjoyment' (DfES 2003).

The impact of NC legislation and the implementation of the National Numeracy Strategy has had an enormous impact on every aspect of mathematics education in school, bringing changes in *what* is taught, as well as *when* and *how*. The primary curriculum is 'packed'. It now challenges teachers to attempt to teach many areas of school mathematics that were traditionally the domain of traditional secondary curriculum. The pressure to complete the 'coverage' of this expanded primary curriculum is explicit and overwhelming. Children's performances in a plethora of tests, constant competition from league tables and the high expectations teachers judge themselves by, influence and inevitably narrow the focus of teaching. With success in SATs as a target for and measure of successful teaching, inevitably children's learning will be about what it is possible to test through such formal assessments. Recent changes to SATs papers have attempted to acknowledge a broader view of mathematics education with the inclusion of more investigative and open-ended challenges. The implicit intention is to influence and change teachers' practice to encourage more creativity in mathematics teaching and learning. Despite this shift in emphasis the assessment of *procedures* remains more manageable and quantifiable than that of *process and application* and *elegance*. As a consequence children's learning is more about facts, skills and knowledge and less concerned with the more creative aspects of mathematics.

Creativity in mathematics

Think for a moment and write down some phrases or words which you would associate with creativity. It may be that you have included some of the following words in your list:

- imagination
- personal
- originality
- flexibility
- freedom
- new ideas
- products
- challenging.

It would be useful to think of examples of these from your own experiences. For example, you may recall a child providing a personal interpretation to a new concept. It may be an instance when a child was driven by curiosity and proposed a personal theory of how a generalisation could be made or asked for extra time to solve a mathematical problem.

Defining creativity is a challenge in itself. We would probably recognise it when we come across it. However, the following definition – from NACCCE – was adopted by Ofsted (2003) and may be useful in guiding practitioners. Creativity is defined as:

Imaginative activity fashioned so as to produce outcomes that are both original and of value. Creative processes have four characteristics. First, they always involve thinking or behaving imaginatively. Second, this innovative activity is purposeful: that is, it is directed to achieve an objective. Third, these processes must generate something original. Fourth, the outcome must be of value in relation to the objective.

(NACCCE 2001: 29)

The key words here are *imagination, purpose, originality* and *value*. *Imagining* a mental number line that is marked in jumps of fives is a creative activity when it is used for the *purpose* of solving a word problem that involves working out the total for nine sets of five sweets. What do we mean by originality? What does it involve in the context of learning mathematics? Is it desirable for children to discover new mathematics principles each time they do mathematics, although it is unlikely? But, if a six-year-old discovers that when you add two odd numbers the answer is always even, or that if we lived in 'spiderland' we would carry numbers in base eight, these are *original* and new ideas for those children and therefore they are being creative. The concept value is a complex one. Value here does not exclude the child. We need to consider whether the child feels something is of *value* and has contributed to his or her learning.

To more fully understand creativity in mathematics it is worth reconstructing your own personal view of the nature of mathematics itself. Consider the following three 'aspects' as a possible means of partitioning different elements of school mathematics:

- procedures
- application
- elegance.

Beginning the task of identification and classification is possibly more important than its completion. The following lists opposite may provide a starting point.

By first considering what constitutes the mathematics curriculum, you are making judgements about *what* elements you consider to be important for children to learn. These choices and decisions allow you to better understand *why* each aspect has a distinct contribution to mathematics education.

Procedures

The most easily identified and explicitly taught elements are those classified as 'procedures'. These might include facts (e.g. number bonds to 10), skills (e.g. measuring lengths with a ruler); and concepts (e.g. understanding the notion of the possibility of an event taking place as being likely or unlikely). These tangible learning outcomes are

Procedures	Application	Elegance
ordering numbers	solving problems	beauty
relationships	solving word problems	mental imagery
calculating with numbers	investigational work	relationships . . .
solving equations	asking questions	connections
measuring	communicating ideas	structure
identifying shapes	hypothesising	efficiency
transforming shapes	predicting	logic
drawing graphs	generalising	patterns
finding probabilities		

well defined within both the National Curriculum for Mathematics and the National Numeracy Strategy.

Application

You may feel that these documents provide less specified details concerning mathematical applications. Progression in the development of children's abilities to use and apply learned procedures is tracked in Attainment Target 1 of the National Curriculum and included in the National Numeracy Strategy explicitly in the solution of real and word problems, and implicitly through examples for learning in each of the identified 'strands'.

Elegance

Recommendations concerning 'elegance' in mathematics teaching and learning are more difficult to find. Yet the National Curriculum in Mathematics (DfES/QCA 1999) reminds us:

> Mathematics is a creative discipline. It can stimulate moments of pleasure and wonder when a pupil solves a problem for the first time, discovers a more elegant solution to that problem, or suddenly sees hidden connections.
>
> (p. 14)

The challenge for teachers goes beyond the intention to extend and strengthen children's *understanding* of the procedures they have learnt and to become better at the process of *applying* the procedures they have learnt in the solution of problems. It extends to the desire for children to make a value judgement about the quality of the method by which the solution is found. The following is an example of a child calculating an answer demonstrating an appreciation of mathematical elegance.

Child A makes a considered choice to solve the question 45 + 28, by adding 30 to 45 and then subtracting 2 from this answer rather than 'partitioning' to adding tens and units. He was able to justify his method because 'it's really easy to add on 30'.

Here the child makes decisions and choices about what would constitute the 'best' method of solving this particular question. Achieving a *speedy* and *accurate* answer necessitates judgements about which strategy would be the most *efficient* and *appropriate* in relation to the specific combination of numbers involved. Success depends on the child's personal experience in a broad range of skills for calculating and expertise in deploying them.

Child B chooses to calculate 32 × 4, by doubling 32 and then doubling this answer. Her reason for calculating the answer in this way is based on the desire to carry out two simpler, well-practised operations rather than risk a mistake in the performance of one more difficult calculation.

In contrast, the appropriateness of a particular solution will be influenced by the child's awareness of relationships between the procedures and applications he/she has learnt; for example, having a 'sense' or 'feel' for numbers and number operations that informs decisions.

Child C calculates the answer to 36 × 25 by multiplying 36 by 100 then dividing by 4. In this instance the child has made a number of connections that link the particular numbers involved in the sum with the fact that 25 × 4 = 100 and the ease by which any number can be multiplied by 100. The method selected is both efficient and appropriate.

In order for children to be able to make informed, personal judgements about the way they work mathematically, teaching and learning must also be concerned with (a) the development of critical thinking and (b) the appreciation of the elegance of mathematics itself. Each aspect – 'procedures', 'applications' and 'elegance' – represents an essential ingredient within mathematics education:

- Children need a stock of learned facts and skills (procedures), so that they can be applied in a variety of contexts and for different purposes;

- Learning to select and use learned facts, skills and concepts (apply) allows children to develop their problem-solving abilities and to strengthen their understanding of the procedures they apply;

- Appreciating interrelationships within mathematics (elegance) enables children to make more informed decisions about the way they apply procedures in order to problem-solve.

Providing opportunities for children to learn in all the defined aspects necessitates introducing children to the more beautiful aspects of mathematics. Aspirations for children's mathematical education goes beyond the purely functional, utilitarian intentions and value learning about creativity within mathematics as an end in itself. It is worth recalling the National Curriculum working party (DfES 1988:13) which stated:

> Mathematics is not only taught because it is useful. It should also be a source of delight and wonder, offering pupils intellectual excitement, for example, in the discovery of relationships, the pursuit of rigour and the achievement of elegant solutions. Pupils should also appreciate the creativity of mathematics.

Mathematics is permeated with logic, patterns and connections. It is these relationships that *structure* and *bind* mathematical knowledge and processes together. As a consequence if you pursue a logical line of mathematical enquiry you will almost certainly enjoy a moment of revelation as you make a connection between two seemingly disparate aspects of your mathematical understanding.

> *Child D practises the addition of strings of numbers. The numbers selected for each addition are even and consecutive (i.e. $2 + 4 + 6 + 8 = 20$ and $4 + 6 + 8 + 10 = 28 \ldots$). The discovery is made that all the answers are multiples of 4. After further investigation the reason for this is found. All the strings of numbers will be composed of two multiples of 4 and two even numbers which are not, but which combine to make another multiple of 4. Since multiplication is repeated addition, the total of two multiples of 4 and pairs of numbers that make a further multiple of 4 will inevitably result in a number that is also divisible by 4.*

In this example the child was allowed to 'invent' his own mathematical relationship. Providing opportunities for children to develop critical thinking also encourages them to think creatively. Furthermore, developing both critical and creative thinking within a curriculum that embraces each of these aspects of mathematics allows children to discover and appreciate the creative nature of mathematics itself. In reviewing our own practice in planning for a rich, creative mathematics education we may ask ourselves these questions:

- Are our pupils experiencing moments of pleasure in their mathematics lessons?

- Are they given opportunities to appreciate creativity in mathematics?

- Are we encouraging our children to explore their own lines of enquiry and make or construct their own personal theories?

Recognising creativity in children's mathematics

All children have some degree of creativity; the issue is how we recognise the creative moments in the classroom. First, creative children are curious; they ask many questions and in some cases challenge ideas put forward by peers, textbooks and teachers. They may put forward an alternate explanation to a mathematical idea or hypothesise a theory. A child learning about the angles of a triangle raised the possibility that if we consider three points on a globe then the sum of the angles is no longer 180 degrees. Such breaking away from a conventional idea and making a new hypothesis is a feature of creativity. You may spot creativity in a child who makes a discovery and attempts a generalisation. Having found a generalised rule, the same child may seek exceptions to this rule.

Another feature of creative behaviour in mathematics may be seen when a child uses a new way of recording something. This may involve a personal form of recording different from that which the teacher advises. Historically, mathematicians who made major intellectual contributions have often created their own symbols and ways of recording.

Children who are creative see connections between mathematical ideas and are able to articulate these clearly and with understanding. In the following example, the teacher asked children to consider the question whether they would like to be a decimal or a fraction. Their contributions exemplify the level of the children's creativity.

> *Heerali began her writing with 'Hello! My name is Dotty and I am a decimal. My family name is 3.33 recurring. My whole family are all the number 3s in different units . . .'.*
>
> *A quite different response came from Shivani, beginning 'Once upon a time in the Land of Maths lived the fractions. They were a happy group and would work with each other. Their sole aim in life was to be part of something. All was well until one day a new group came to town. Terrified they made a mighty army of numerators and denominators. We all know that there are an infinite number of fractions and so they were quite confident they would be able to defeat their sworn enemies . . .'*

If you study the above examples, you will see that these contributions not only show the use of imagination; they also give us an insight into the level of their understanding. By undertaking such tasks, we can enable children to make connections and enhance their understanding. In departing from routine textbook pages of exercises, requiring children to convert fractions into decimals, in order to pose a more creative question, the children were given a more worthwhile and enjoyable means of developing their understanding of relationships between fractions and a decimal. Given such opportunities children often respond imaginatively to 'what if . . .' kinds of questions. The following are examples of questions that have encouraged children to think more creatively:

- What would happen if all the rulers disappeared?
- Imagine if there were no standard measures?
- What if the key 6 of the calculator was broken? How would you use it to calculate 369 + 674?

■ What if you won £600 to refurnish your bedroom and were given a catalogue to choose from?

In all these contexts children are offered opportunities to generate original ideas, select different pathways and make decisions. The processes of reasoning, refining, estimating and making decisions should also contribute to greater mathematical understanding.

Children who are creative often possess metacognitive abilities and are able to stand back and make an assessment of the quality of a piece of work. Most enjoy the challenge of creating a mathematical game with an unusual set of rules. They respond positively to comparing two types of mathematical resources, whether it be two mathematical games or how two different textbooks introduce the operation of division.

Strategies for encouraging creativity in mathematics

Identifying and encouraging creativity are parts of a two-way process. It is unlikely that a teacher will spot creative behaviour if children are not provided with opportunities to be creative. In the same way, it is only by providing creative experiences that a teacher can begin to understand what and how to promote creativity. So how can the teacher encourage children to be creative? In our attempts to foster creativity the following strategies are worthy of consideration.

Providing a creative working environment

Fostering creative ways of working

Lift the constraints of time when a child is motivated and engaged in an activity. Discuss the lives of well-known mathematicians who pursued a task for months and years before they produced worthwhile contributions for posterity.

Allowing children to pursue creative ideas

Allow freedom within the learning objectives for children to make use of original ideas. This requires teachers to give pupils the freedom to select their own pathways of enquiry and to both accept and value unexpected outcomes.

Developing creative thinking through questioning

Ask open-ended questions which enable children to offer different types of responses and perspectives, instead of closed questions, which elicit short answers. To enable children to invent with original ideas, instead of asking children to multiply 4 × 3 ask them to give you an unusual sum that gives the answer 12. Rather than questioning children about the name of a shape, suggest they draw a particular shape. Value thinking rather than memory by using phrases like 'How is it that . . .?'; 'What if . . .?; 'Can you think of a different way . . .?'.

Encouraging creativity in the way ideas are recorded

Encourage children to choose creative ways of recording using diagrams, cartoons and speech bubbles to present mathematical ideas. Think carefully about the purposes of the children's recording. Ensure that it contributes to their learning and the development of their ideas. For example, structuring their thinking, keeping track of information and communicating ideas.

Presenting a creative role model

Use a variety of teaching styles and take into account children's learning styles.

Plan for children to work in mixed- and same-ability groups as well as independently on a variety of different types of activities. Let children experiment with different practical resources that provide them with 'tools to think with'. Use equipment such as arrow cards, multilink and money to structure and support the development of ideas and strengthen understanding. Be inventive in the way you present ideas using different approaches and contexts to challenge and intrigue children. Introduce work in the form of a game, puzzle or perhaps a story. Increase children's independence by allowing them to follow their own lines of enquiry. Encourage them to generate their own examples by picking up cards, throwing dice, selecting arrow cards or using spinners rather than tackling worksheets.

The following examples show a child's developing ideas as they worked in a classroom that encouraged creativity.

> *Children were shown a number of 'consecutive sums', so called because each sum was made up of consecutive numbers (e.g. 2 + 3 and 9 + 10, 21 + 22 etc. From this starting point Helen quickly went on to discover that any two consecutive numbers will result in an odd answer and to explain the reason why.*

Because all the numbers go odd, even, odd all the sums will have an odd and an even number. When you add an odd and an even and an even and an odd the answers must be all odd.

FIGURE 5.1

> *Given the encouragement, time and freedom to explore her own questions she went on to investigate the notion of consecutive sums in greater depth. Having continued the work at home and during the following lesson she made a number of other discoveries.*

If you add three consecutive numbers the awnser is always in the three times table

(e.g) 1+2+3 = 6 = 3 times table → three times two
10+11+12=33=3 times table → three times eveven
4+5+6 = 15 = 3 times table → three times five
} because one number more and one number is less

FIGURE 5.2

Her personal achievement was a result of being given the opportunity to work creativity.

Planning for creative teaching and learning

Providing creative starting points for learning

Identify opportunities to be creative in the planning stage by selecting activities that provide children with choices and multiple pathways of enquiry. These activities support, rather than replace, lessons that target teaching of facts and skills. It is unlikely that children can be engaged in creative explorations if they do not possess a storehouse of knowledge and mental fluency. However, providing opportunities to select and apply learned procedures strengthens understanding, develops thinking skills and allows children to develop positive attitudes and an appreciation of mathematical elegance. The following activity from school is such an example:

> *Barbara, a Year 4 teacher, chose the context of Smarties for encouraging her children to learn data handling and at the same time to be creative. The objective of the lesson was to use what they had learned about handling data – sorting, classifying, constructing charts, frequency tables, as well as to be engaged in problem-solving and posing their own problems. Rather than use a textbook exercise she chose a context which motivated pupils and allowed them opportunities for originality and freedom of enquiry. The session started with the teacher holding up a few tubes of Smarties and asking the children to think of questions they would like to investigate. Questions came rapidly:*

- *How many Smarties are there in a tube?*
- *How many colours are there?*
- *Are there the same number of Smarties in all the tubes?*
- *Are the colours equally distributed? How can we show this?*
- *What are the ingredients on a Smarties tube? How are these expressed?*

- *What is the weight of a Smarty?*

- *Is the tube the best container for Smarties?*

- *Is there a relation between the colour of the lid and the content of the tube?*

- *Is there any significance in the letter on the lid of the tube?*

Barbara asked groups of children to investigate the questions and choose the best form of recording to communicate it to others. Children were highly motivated. All the facts and skills they had been taught were applied. Many creative ways of recording findings were produced. One group produced a book with the title: 'Only Smarties have the answers', with a variety of colourful diagrams and graphs. Some children posed more questions as their curiosity was aroused. This very creative lesson with a high level of learning outcomes, was the result of Barbara's appropriate choice of a motivating context.

Providing resources to support creative thinking

Use resources to allow children to work more independently and follow their own lines of enquiry. Carefully selected and designed resources improve the quality of children's learning in a number of ways providing:

(i)   clarification, meaning and structure (e.g. placing work in a real context with money or developing ideas by playing a game);

(ii) purpose, motivation and enjoyment (e.g. allowing children to generate their own examples to work on by throwing dice or selecting cards);

(iii) 'tools to think with' (e.g. developing children's understanding of ordering or classifying by having the opportunity to actually physically move and rearrange apparatus); and

(iv) means of modelling personal theories and ideas (e.g. challenging children to use equipment, illustrate and prove their discoveries).

The following problem-solving activity, 'Squaring up to the Problem', was originally designed for higher ability children but has been used with children of a wide ability range in order to develop their knowledge and ideas about shape and space.

Children are given a 6cm × 6cm square of expensive golden fabric. This represents the size and shape of their current school badge background. Their brief is to design a new badge background that has the same area as the original shape. The design must be created by cutting the square of fabric into two identical pieces and then rearranging them to form a new shape. Initially, two ways of doing this can be shown with some examples of how these could be rearranged:

One cut horizontally or vertically

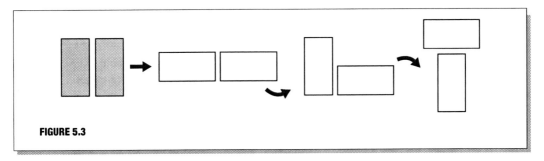

FIGURE 5.3

And an alternative cut diagonally

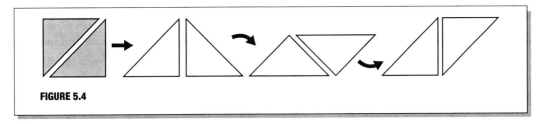

FIGURE 5.4

Once children fully understand the challenge they can begin to investigate and design practically. Having the opportunity to cut, rearrange and paste lots of different possible badge designs provides children with many opportunities to think creatively about their understanding in the topic of shape and space. Encouraging children to find mathematical terms or invent their own names for each of the new shapes they create reveals a great deal about their understanding of the shapes and their properties. Furthermore, the generation of quantities of different shapes, which all have the same area, provides a powerful means of reinforcing the concept of the conservation of area.

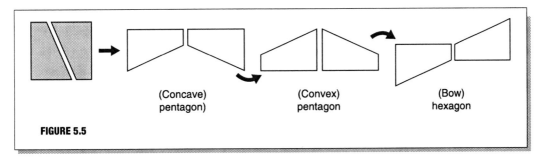

(Concave)
pentagon)

(Convex)
pentagon

(Bow)
hexagon

FIGURE 5.5

As children explore different designs they can be challenged to evaluate and refine their thinking still further. Providing them with the head teacher's requirements for the badge requires them to evaluate and justify their designs:

- *to accommodate the school logo the badge shape must have at least one line of symmetry;*

- *in order to reduce wastage of the expensive material being used, the badge shape should tessellate;*

- *the outline of the badge should be easily and quickly sewn on school jackets.*

As children create shapes and collect information about each design, they are striving to find the 'best' design by thinking inventively about each of the criteria outlined in the design brief. Ideas about symmetry, tessellation and perimeter can be more fully explored by physically moving, rearranging, sorting, classifying, folding, turning, comparing and contrasting resources.

The activity provided an opportunity for children to work creatively and illustrates how children can benefit from working practically. Having the opportunity to work kinaesethically improves the quality of:

- children's work – when children are engaged in design the possibilities of new and re-warding connections are allowed between existing knowledge and understanding. Inevitably it brings a new dimension to previous learning;

- teacher's teaching and assessments – observing children working with resources reveals a 'window' into their thinking, providing insights that allow misconceptions to be addressed and more accurate assessment of achievements and abilities to be made.

Conclusion

All children have the potential to be creative, but creative outcomes will only occur if the teacher fosters the innate creativity in the child. The challenge for the teacher is to both plan to provide creativity in learning experiences as well as being receptive to the development of the child's natural creativity. Planning involves the teacher considering the possibilities for children to engage in the creative that permeates mathematics itself through each aspect of the mathematics curriculum; procedures, process and applica-tion; and elegance. These experiences are more fully developed within a learning environment that values creativity in mathematics. In a classroom where only correct answers are valued, curiosity is stifled and there is very little room to be creative. In many of the examples given in this chapter it is clear that when the teacher uses his or her own creativity, children respond creatively.

The following words from Casey (1999), 'Caged birds do sing, but what would be their song if they are sometimes allowed to fly', reflect current ideas about what is important in mathematics education. It is not sufficient for children to be taught to be competent learners of mathematics. There is a drive for children to not only enjoy the creative aspects of mathematics but also to become creative in their own work as mathematicians. It will be difficult for teachers to plan for creativity and enjoyment while meeting all the expectations imposed by curriculum coverage and assessment targets. However, if children are able to unlock the creativity within themselves, and the subject itself, they could develop a fascination for mathematics that extends beyond the classroom. We believe that creativity can coexist within the structure of the National Curriculum and the NNS. How this is achieved will ultimately depend on the creativity of the teacher.

Further reading

Casey, R. (1999) 'A Key Concept model for teaching and learning mathematics in school'. *The Mathematics Association*, 28(3).

DfEE (1988) *Mathematics in the National Curriculum*. London: DfEE.

DfES (2003) *Excellence and Enjoyment*. London: DfES.

DfES/QCA (1999) *Mathematics: The National Curriculum in England and Wales*. London: DfES.

Koshy, V. and Murray, J. (2000) *Unlocking Numeracy*. London: David Fulton.

National Advisory Committee on Creative and Cultural Education (NACCCE) (2001) *All Our Futures: Creativity and Education*. London: DfES.

Ofsted (2003) Expecting the Unexpected HMI (www.ofsted.gov.uk).

Creativity in science: leaping the void

Juliet Edmonds

'I think the water in the puddle has disappeared because a big black dog came along and drank it all up.'

(Gita, aged 6)

THIS MAY NOT BE the exact answer on evaporation that the teacher was expecting yet it is a credible and creative explanation as to how water disappears from puddles in the street. Gita had made a leap between knowing dogs need water to live, that puddles contain water and that puddles seem to get smaller over time if the weather stays dry, to suggest a hypothesis. It is those very leaps that scientists create to provide models of our natural and physical world.

There is a public belief that science gains its credibility from the objectivity of scientific methodology. Scientific knowledge tends to hold a hallowed position in our society at present, partly due to the belief that this objectivity provides knowledge which is somehow superior and more valid than other methods of obtaining knowledge (Ziman 1968). The idea that scientists use this objective method and are methodical in their exploration of the natural and physical world appears to exclude the idea of creativity. Following a methodological process seems to be seen to exclude the activity of making leaps of imagination and the process of originality. Yet this view of science neglects to note that scientists have devised hypotheses to be tested in the first place. Having carried out extensive, meticulous research which often involves a creative process of making links to previous science knowledge, they then generalise the research to a range of situations, coming up with possible explanation of patterns in data.

There are many examples of this process: Darwin and Wallace making hypotheses on the process of evolution heretically contrary to the then current belief on creationism; Watson and Crick 'playing' with their cardboard base pairs to try and find a model that would explain the results of X-ray crystallography pictures. They all provided solutions to problems that were different to those within the prevailing paradigm of scientific belief. Philosophers such as Thomas Kuhn would argue that these leaps of the imagination are the very way that scientific knowledge progresses. He suggests that current paradigms of scientific belief are destabilised through such 'scientific revolutions'; then the ultimate replacement of an old paradigm with a new one follows (Kuhn 1970). This suggests that progression in science depends on creative leaps and links to unexpected knowledge. I recently heard a polymer scientist on the radio discussing how he went into the wrong room at a conference centre and found links, and inspiration, between the application of string theory in astrophysics to his own work and vice versa.

All these scientists surely fulfil the criteria from the National Advisory Committee for Creativity and Culture in Education Report commissioned by the DfEE that the characteristics of creativity involve

'thinking or behaving *imaginatively*. Second, overall this imaginative activity is *purposeful*: that is, it is directed to achieving an objective. Third, these processes must generate something *original*. Fourth, the outcome must be of *value* in relation to the objective.'

(NACCCE 1999)

Teachers' attitudes to creativity in primary science

Ideas about the role of science in our society are reflected in teachers' ideas about science in the classroom. It is often the case that primary teachers believe that creativity is linked to the arts and not the sciences (Feasey 2003) and their own level of subject knowledge and attitudes to science can result in teaching styles that foster or destroy creativity.

There are a number of actions and attitudes displayed by teachers in classrooms which influence children's science. Primary science causes some teachers specific problems, particularly those who lack accuracy and confidence in their own subject knowledge. Researchers have found many teachers' ideas of everyday occurrences to be similar to those of the children they teach (Kruger *et al.* 1989). Many of the alternative frameworks held by teachers about electricity and current are the same models used by children of about 7–11 years of age. This does not have to stifle creativity within a classroom but it certainly affects the confidence levels of teachers which, in turn, affects their chosen teaching methods and emphasis on knowledge over process (Littledyke 1997).

Teachers lacking confidence in their own science knowledge have been found to teach using more didactic teaching methods than other teachers. They tend to avoid discussion and are often unable to focus children's thinking (Lee 1995; Tobin and Fraser 1990). Teaching strategies that enable children to think to solve problems are often more likely to foster creativity in science than those which portray science as a set of facts in a dusty textbook.

However, it appears that this situation is gradually improving. Ofsted recently reported that Initial Teacher Training is very effective in preparing students to teach science, and science learning centres are being set up around the country to continue the support for teachers in school (Ofsted 2002). There is now a range of accessible books on science subject knowledge for primary teachers that concentrate on the teacher's understanding, as opposed to GCSE textbooks which often have an emphasis on mathematical modelling.[1]

Although there may be problems with teachers' own attitudes to science, the aims, processes and current pedagogical paradigm on developing conceptual understanding makes the subject an excellent context for creativity in the primary classroom, as will now be shown.

Creativity and the aims of Primary Science Education

When Harlen (2000) identifies the aims of primary science education we can see that science can be a highly creative process.[2] She builds on the aims suggested in the National Curriculum for science and suggests that as primary teachers we are aiming to – among other skills – develop process skills in science – including prediction and hypothesis; planning; considering evidence; and evaluation – develop attitudes – including willingness to change ideas; critical reflection; and curiosity – and start to develop current concepts to explain our natural and physical world. All these aims have potential for developing creative thought and activity. The potential of each will be considered in turn.

Children's development of process skills can provide a unique opportunity to think of alternative ideas, methods and solutions.

Prediction and raising hypotheses

Prediction of the outcome of an investigation can allow children to think of, and work through, alternative outcomes. A hypothesis is a more sophisticated form of prediction where an outcome is suggested based on prior experience or scientific knowledge. This allows the child to make links to previous understanding and also to make imaginative leaps to alternative outcomes that could occur. This stage of the exploratory process can be an important time for discussion about possible outcomes of investigations. Some children are so convinced by their predictions that they can carry out theory-led data-gathering. For example, when investigating whether the human cubit was the same length as the foot size I watched one child take the measurement of another child's foot with a tape measure, then, without letting go of the measurement on the tape, place it on the child's cubit and confirm it was the same! He carried on using the same method for all the children in his sample and then confirmed that his prediction had been correct all along.

Planning and evaluating investigations

Planning and evaluating investigations allows children to suggest a variety of ways of testing their hypotheses and to explore the notion of controlling variables. Even if children suggest inappropriate methods for testing their hypotheses, the dialogue between the teacher and the child can lead to greater understanding of fair testing or investigation. Prompting children to consider other ways in which hypotheses could be tested before or after investigative work can also extend children's thinking about planning. The use of planning boards, writing frames and teacher prompts can be helpful for taking children through the process for planning investigations.[3]

Considering evidence

Considering evidence is a time where children can interpret patterns in data or observations. There is much potential here for a variety of forms of creative thinking; making meaningful links with previous learning, applying previous learning to a new situation, making generalisations to apply to a range of different situations from the present, and suggesting explanations of observed patterns. Children could even be involved in forming theoretical models to explain the evidence – for example, using toy cars in a dual carriageway filtering down to one lane, modelling the effect of electrons travelling through a fine light bulb element.

Willingness to change ideas

Harlen's aims for developing scientific attitudes could also encourage the use of creative thought through fostering a willingness to change ideas. It would seem that a precursor to this would be a willingness to consider a range of ideas. A strategy to encourage this skill is to look at alternative explanations of events. For example, when water in a puddle appeared to disappear and the class believed the water was sucked up from the ground, the teacher asked the children to suggest a range of alternative theories on where the water had gone. The class set up investigations to explore each of the theories and looked at which one best fitted the evidence. After watching a puddle on a black plastic bag the children concluded that the water could not have 'gone into the earth'.

Critical reflection

Critical reflection is also an important skill to check that imaginative ideas are 'purposeful' and 'useful'. Curiosity also can be the motivation behind thinking and trying out new solutions to problems. Developing a questioning classroom through the collection of questions, teachers modelling questions, databases of questions, and recording questions in notebooks while investigating, can be a first step in allowing curiosity to flourish in a classroom.

Examples of fostering creativity through science exploration

While working with an inner-London school on non-fiction writing, an opportunity for exploring creative hypotheses and model-making arose. I was working with a Year 6 class who had recently finished their SATs. The school was offering an enhancement programme to children before they left in the summer. They had studied chemical and physical change in science the previous term and had recently attended 'Junior Citizen',[4] a multi-agency initiative including the emergency services, that offered training for Key Stage 2 pupils, so we decided to set them a problem. I used a situation that had been posed to teachers on a CLIS (Children's Learning in Science[5] course, run by Leeds University, where three candles of equal height were left burning under a bell jar. The candles were placed in a line with one in the middle of the jar and the others at either side. The children were given the task of predicting what might happen and why, and of testing their ideas by moving and replacing candles. The candles and bell jar were set in a sand tray to conform to health and safety guidelines. I remembered that the course leaders had suggested that it was just as possible for a child to come up with an answer as a university lecturer!

We started the session by asking the children about their subject knowledge from their topic on 'change' and also what they had learned about fire and heat during their 'Junior Citizen' training. We asked the children to predict what might happen to the candles in the bell jar when they had been lit. The children's ideas were recorded on the whiteboard. We lit the candles and watched the sequence of events. The children were surprised when first one outer candle then the other went out and the middle candle continued to burn for a while. We asked the children to come up with alternative patterns or ways to test the candles so we could find out more about why it had happened. The children were excited and kept coming up with new hypotheses about why the candle snuffing pattern was occurring. These hypotheses were often to do with the length of the wick of each candle or the order of lighting. This also provided the opportunity to explore ideas on fair testing through discussion on whether it was fair to use the same candles in a new pattern, some of which were now shorter than others.

We got through rather a lot of candles during that lesson! The session also necessitated a great deal of new vocabulary. Children were asked to explain terms such as 'oxygen' and 'convection'. The children finally went away in groups, having explored a number of candle permutations in the jar, and argued and finalised their own explanation and theories on what was happening inside the bell jar. Many drew large diagrams showing air movements inside the jar. Some children showed great creative thinking in their explanations. They demonstrated original thought, albeit based on knowledge they had built up through their learning and own experiences on the 'Junior Citizen' course where they had to escape from a smoke-filled room. The models helped the children to understand why the smoke and air behave in a certain manner. Little of the activity could be said to be covering the National Curriculum for Science (DfEE 1999) but meaningful, relevant learning and creative thinking were going on. The children commented that they felt they were acting like 'real' scientists; 'discovering things for the first time' (Natalie, aged 11).

Another strategy using the development of process skills to develop creative thinking is a kind of science workshop based on the writing workshop format.[6] The children collect a number of science questions that arise in everyday life, during class investigations or other science work, or from children's personal interest. These questions were saved in each child's notebook. The teacher then sets aside time when these questions could be investigated, providing support for identifying questions that could be ethically and

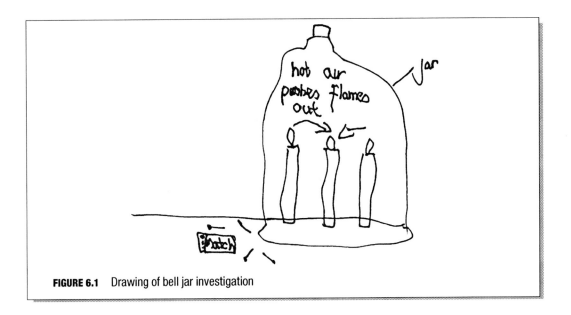

FIGURE 6.1 Drawing of bell jar investigation

viably investigated, planning, carrying out and evaluating evidence and methods. This allows opportunities for children to develop their own curiosity about the natural and physical world and gives children the chance to explore their own understanding and form their own, sometimes creative, ideas about the world. Some examples of questions for investigation were: 'Do square bubble blowers make square bubbles?'; 'Can woodlice swim?' and 'Can children with longer legs run faster?'.

Developing creativity through conceptual understanding

The aim of primary science education is to develop current concepts that explain the natural and physical world. Therefore, there could be conflict between this and allowing children to use their creativity to form their ideas about the world. However, current thinking in science education states that it is ineffective to 'tell' children science ideas. The constructivist approach to learning in science recognises that children are active learners and that they will take on board ideas which are congruent with their own mental frameworks to describe their world but will often reject current scientific ideas if they are in conflict with their thinking (Osborne and Freyberg 1985). Curriculum materials such as the Nuffield Primary Science (1995) advocate allowing children to explore their own alternative frameworks and then provide a range of experiences to encourage the children to alter their frameworks in line with current scientific thinking. The research that influenced the development of Nuffield science recognised that although this is a more effective method of helping children to understand science, it is often limited in its success as many children's alternative frameworks are persistent and last into adulthood. Nevertheless, exploring children's ideas in science provides opportunities for creative thinking through the creation of theories and models to describe the world.

Examples of creative thinking about the natural and physical world

Children's thinking about their world constantly surprises. I was working with a Year 5 class investigating what makes the best cup of tea: type of teabag, loose or bagged, stirred or not stirred. Two girls quickly made it obvious that their curiosity lay in a different direction; they were interested in how teabags work. This may sound obvious to you or me, but there were some interesting alternative frameworks driving these children's actions. They were influenced by an advertising campaign that boasted the superior design of the holes in a specific company's teabags. The girls completed a planning sheet and carefully proceeded to cover the holes in one tea bag with overlapping strips of sticky tape and planned a fair test using the same amounts and temperature of water. Not surprisingly, the tape shrivelled off the teabag immediately it was put into the hot water. I encouraged the girls to try another method of testing their teabag. They came back very proudly with the results of their labour; a teabag inside a knotted plastic bag. I had to bite my tongue not to comment on this. I was astounded that the girls actually expressed surprise that the 'bagged' teabag did not colour the water at all. They obviously had some interesting ideas about permeability and materials and were willing to explore them using a variety of methods. At this point I gave the girls some magnifying glasses and asked them to look very carefully at the surface of the teabag. It would have been interesting to pursue these children's thinking further. Although their thinking may not have contributed to the class investigation they were certainly developing skills and curiosity that would encourage their creative thinking in the future.

There is always the temptation, even after sessions of exploratory investigative work, such as the above, to sit the children down and tell them that their ideas were interesting but this is 'the real scientific view'. This tends to promote science as a set of facts and negates the view of science as a way of working. In support of this, many of my science education students report that the most significant learning for them in secondary science was how to fiddle the results of your experiment to fit the expectation of the teacher and then to regurgitate the conclusion stated by the teacher for homework! More creative strategies for drawing together the knowledge and understanding in the lesson are sessions where the teacher draws out the similarities and differences between the children's ideas and that of the current scientific views, or where the emphasis is on 'explanatory stories', where the teacher looks at a variety of stories from the children and from current science practice, making links between various bits of science artificially atomised by National Curriculum and planning structures (Millar and Osborne 1998).

Metaphors, analogies and creativity

Sutton (1996) identified the importance of creating metaphors and analogies as one part of science enquiry and sometimes the first stage in forming new scientific theories. He quotes the nineteenth-century scientist Faraday who was convinced that modelling was one of the initial stages in forming scientific theories. Faraday suggested that this modelling stage came before the scientific investigation and that the model was then rejected or modified in light of the scientific evidence. Watson and Crick used this method, creating models of the constituents of DNA and experimenting with a model of a structure, trying out the models with X-ray crystallography images as well as talking to chemists about the chemical forms possible in DNA and drawing on previous research on the amounts of the various constituents in the structure. After a number of false starts they found a model that agreed with all the currently held data on DNA and also a structure which provided a possible explanation of how DNA replicates itself. Watson's own awe and wonder is evident in his own account of the modelling. He was concerned that the structure would turn out to be boring, but to his delight it seemed beautiful and perfectly designed for its function (Watson 1970).

If this is the way scientific thinking can develop perhaps we need to spend more time allowing children to create and explore their own models of such things as electrical current, convection and so on, instead of making them conform to standard models and analogies – it will not only allow them to be more creative in their thinking but it will also replicate the ways in which scientists work.

Fostering a creative science classroom

Teachers and their classroom ethos are pivotal in producing creativity in science. In Chapter 1, Robert Fisher states that creative children are stimulated by creative teachers. As discussed previously, the actions and attitudes of teachers are inherited from their own experiences and training. Teachers need to be aware of their own limitations and look critically at the ethos of their classroom to establish what actions can be taken to develop a 'creative classroom'. We all need to look at the roles played by teachers and children in each subject. In which subjects do we encourage discussion and divergent thought? In which subjects do we control the talking and responses of the children? In which subjects do we tolerate divergent thought? What are our own experiences of science and what messages are we passing on to the class about science?

Science in a creative classroom needs to be portrayed less as a set body of facts and more as shifting, explanatory stories. It is more about a way of working than about resultant knowledge that can only ever be provisional. In light of this view of science, teachers could value and respect children's alternative frameworks of the world however inconsistent they are with the current scientific thinking. After all, these ideas have done a fairly good job of allowing children to function in their physical world to date. Of course, we have a responsibility to help children encounter experiences that will challenge and help them reform their ideas, but without stamping out the idea that there can often be a range of viewpoints and theories on the same subject.

This open approach can be reinforced by developing a *thinking* classroom in which even the teacher's ideas can be questioned. In an account and analysis of two primary teacher's experiences of introducing *Let's Think through Science* (Adey *et al.* 2003) – a programme of developing thinking skills and metacognition in science – to their classrooms, it became apparent that there was a major shift in the language the teachers used in the classroom and how they envisaged their role (Ambrose 2003). They radically altered the style of their lessons, the way they asked questions and the amount they interjected in the group work. Many of the tasks carried out had no set answer so everyone's opinion had a value. The project was highly beneficial in getting children to think creatively, not only in science, but also across the whole curriculum.

Teacher questioning styles can also have a huge effect on thinking in science classrooms. Asking person- rather than subject-centred questions allows children to express their own thoughts and discourages a 'guess what the teacher is thinking' style of teaching. For example, 'What do you think will happen next?' rather than 'What will the car do down the higher slope?' avoids implying there is only one correct answer (Harlen 2000; Jelly 1985).

Developing a type of discourse in science where children's ideas and predictions and methods are discussed can be helpful. Feasey reports that 20 per cent of teachers thought that dialogue was a key strategy for increasing creativity by conscious effort; another 20 per cent cited practical activities and problem-solving (Feasey 2003). Teachers use different language according to the subject matter and their beliefs about the subject (Edwards and Mercer 1987). If we project a view of science as knowledge only available from books, rather than a way of modelling and exploring our natural and physical world, the result will be to stifle any exploration of the child's own thoughts and explanations. We need to set up discussions where the class and teacher explore currently held ideas in science and their surroundings in a practical exploratory manner, where the teacher can be questioned and where the child does not fear being questioned.

More importantly, we need to allow children time to explore and think about what they have found in a supportive, relaxed environment. Neurologists have found that we often have creative, original thoughts but we lose them in a mass of other information being processed by our brains. It will be familiar to all how many more innovative ideas we have when we have time and are relaxed – when on holiday for example. Children also need relaxed time at school. This seems unlikely in the pressured environment of our primary schools where every minute of the teacher-led literacy and numeracy sessions are accounted for and where teachers and children are under pressure to produce results. Perhaps in science, if we resist mimicking the controlled teaching style of these strategies, we can allow children the space, confidence, practical experiences and time to think, and thereby allow them to be truly creative.

Notes

1   Useful books for developing teacher's subject knowledge in science: Devereux, J. (2000) *Developing Primary Subject Knowledge in Science*, PCP; or Wenham, M. (1995) *Understanding Primary Science*, PCP.

2 Useful primary science text: Harlen, W. (2000) (3rd edn) *The Teaching of Science in Primary Schools*. London: David Fulton.

3 For a range of writing frames to support the planning of investigations and recording in science see Nuffield (1998) *Science and Literacy: A Guide for Teachers*. Collins.

4 Contact your local police authority for information about 'Junior Citizen' training courses.

5 The work of the CLIS project is described in Driver, R. *et al.* (1994) *Making Sense of Secondary Science: Research into Children's Ideas*, Routledge. Nuffield Primary Science draws on the SPACE research on children's ideas in primary schools (see www.nuffield.org.uk).

6 For more information on writing workshops see Wyse, D. (1998) *Primary Writing*. Open University Press.

Further reading

Adey, P., Serret, N., Robertson, W. and Nagy, F. (2003) *Let's Think through Science*. NFER-Nelson.

Ambrose, J. and Edmondson, R. (2003) *Let's Think in Year 1*. Presented at the Cognitive Acceleration Convention 2003 at the Hilton Hotel, Paddington.

DfEE (2000) *The National Curriculum Handbook for Primary Teachers in England Key Stage 1 and 2*: London: QCA.

Edwards, D. and Mercer, N. (1987) *Common Knowledge*. London: Routledge.

Feasey, R. (2003) 'Creative futures', in ASE, *Primary Science Review*, 78, May/June.

Harlen, W. (2000) *The Teaching of Science in Primary Schools* (3rd edn). London: David Fulton.

Jelly, S. (1985) 'Helping children to raise questions – and answering them', in Harlen, W. (ed.) *Primary Science: Taking the Plunge*. London: Heinemann.

Kruger, C., Summers, M. and Palacio, D. (1989) 'INSET for primary science in the National Curriculum in England and Wales: Are the real needs of teachers perceived?' *Journal for Education in Teaching*, 16(2).

Kuhn, T. (1970) *The Structure of Scientific Revolutions*. Chicago: University of Chicago Press.

Lee, O. (1995) 'Subject matter knowledge, classroom management and instructional practices in middle school science classrooms'. *Journal of Research in Science Teaching*, 32(4).

Littledyke, M. (1997) 'Science education for environmental awareness'. Paper presented at the Third Summer Conference for Teacher Education in Primary Science, University of Durham, July.

Millar, R. and Osborne, J. (eds) (1998) *Beyond 2000 Science Education for the Future*. London: King's College.

National Advisory Committee on Creative and Cultural Education (NACCCE) (1999) *All our Futures: Creativity, Culture and Education*. London: DfEE.

Nuffield (1995) *Primary Science*. London: Collins Educational.

Ofsted (2002) *Science in Primary Initial Training*. London: HMSO.

Osborne, R. and Freyberg, P. (1985) *Learning in Science: the Implications of Children's Science*. London: Heinemann.

Sutton, C (1996) 'Beliefs about science and beliefs about language'. *International Journal of Science Education*, 18(1).

Tobin, K. and Fraser, B. (1990) 'What does it mean to be an exemplary science teacher?' *Journal of Research in Science Teaching*, 27(1).

Watson, J. (1970) *The Double Helix*. London: Penguin.

Ziman, J. (1968) *Public Knowledge*. Cambridge: Cambridge University Press.

Unlocking creativity with ICT

Avril Loveless and Rupert Wegerif

'Computers are useless. They can only give you answers.'

(Pablo Picasso)

'When art and technology come together, magical things happen.'

(Andy Cunningham[1])

Introduction

IF WE COMPARE ICT to drama, music, art or English it is clear that it is not one of the subjects that has traditionally been most closely associated with creativity. Perhaps this is not surprising. ICT is a subject that is seen as focusing on computers, and computers are essentially rule-following machines. If the output of a computer is not predictable from the input then there is usually something wrong with it. However, much the same could be said about a pencil, but this does not lead us to say that pencils are uncreative tools. Computers are different from other educational resources because they tend to be treated as if they were in some way like people, as can be seen in the quotation above from Picasso. A computer with a drawing package can be used in a similar way to a pencil. Picasso did not say that his pencils were useless so why did he say this about computers? The point is not that computers are really like Delphic oracles – just giving answers to our questions, as Picasso seemed to think – nor, on the other hand, like mere pencils recording our movements, but that they can be made to act in many different ways and used to support many different kinds of activity. This means that educators have a responsibility to decide how they want to use them to serve specific educational aims. Picasso is perhaps right in one way – computers are useless on their own, but with the addition of the professional expertise and foresight of teachers they can be put to use to provide spaces for the flowering of pupil's creativity within the curriculum.

In this chapter we will look at the particular ways in which the characteristics of ICT, and the ICT curriculum, fit together with the goal of teaching children to be creative. However, we also want to stress that it is not just the characteristics of ICT, or particular software, that determine any educational activity but how ICT is used by teachers and children to support the learning process. To illustrate the importance of the way that the teacher sets the task, we start this chapter with one example where the relationship between the ICT content and the learning experience was fairly oblique and yet where it is clear that the ICT content was used to stimulate the imaginations of many children.

The Blue Peter challenge

Robotics is very much a part of the ICT curriculum but this often, in practice, means little more than programming Roamers to negotiate floorplans. With the popularity of robots on television and high sales of quite advanced robot kits to parents, it might be worth schools becoming a little more adventurous. In 2002, the BBC children's programme Blue Peter issued a challenge to children to design really useful robots.[2] This generated many highly original ideas and beautiful drawings to illustrate them. For example, the first prize in the seven-and-under group went to Steven Sutton for his caterpillar robot to wake you up in the morning.

This imaginative and appealing design has now been converted, with the help of the RoboFesta team, into a working prototype. The winning designs in the other age groups were no less imaginative. The 8–10 prize, for example, was won by Poppy Mosbacher,

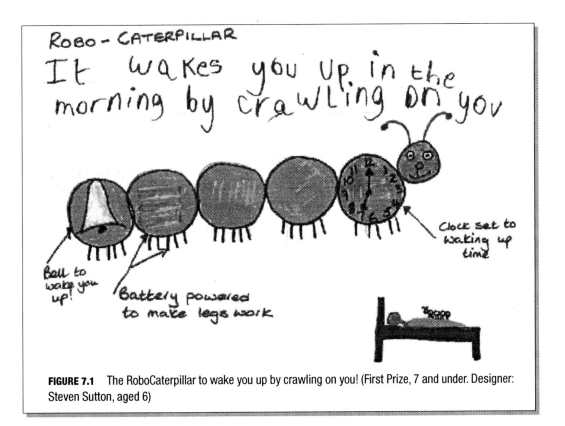

FIGURE 7.1 The RoboCaterpillar to wake you up by crawling on you! (First Prize, 7 and under. Designer: Steven Sutton, aged 6)

aged 8, who actually built her 'PaintPal Robot' to help paint walls, and sent in an annotated photograph rather than a drawing. The 11–15 prize was won by Joel Pitt, aged 13, for a very professional looking design for a solar-powered robot that could move along railtracks in front of trains and detect hairline cracks in the iron rails. Although this high-profile international competition was a one-off event the 'RoboFesta-UK' (http://robofesta.open.ac.uk/) association continues to organise events where groups of children build robots together, often in competition with other groups, with many schools participating.

How ICT can support creativity

The majority of the 32,000 designs received in the RoboFesta competition were never built but were inspired by the idea of robots. This illustrates that ICT can be used to support creativity in oblique as well as direct ways. Depending on how it is taught, ICT can be at the creative cutting-edge, and this is where most young people want to be. But as well as having the potential to inspire the imagination, are there other, more distinctive, features of ICT that can support creativity? What are the characteristics of digital technologies, if any, that offer a distinctive contribution to creative activities that might be different from other tools or media? Are there features of these information and communication technologies that can be exploited to do things that could not be done as effectively, or at all, using other tools? And does the creative use of ICT provide opportunities for the interaction between these features, children's general 'ICT capability' and creative processes? Each of these questions will now be explored more fully.

Distinctive features of digital technologies that support creativity

We think that there are distinctive features of ICT that can support creativity and they can be described as follows: 'provisionality', 'interactivity', 'capacity', 'range', 'speed', 'accuracy', 'quality', 'automation', 'multi-modality', 'neutrality' and 'social credibility'. The *provisionality* of ICT enables users to make changes, try out alternatives and keep a 'trace' of the development of ideas. *Interactivity* engages users at a number of levels, from the playing of a game that gives feedback on decisions made, to the monitoring of a space probe through immediate and dynamic feedback. ICT demonstrates *capacity* and *range* in the ways in which it affords access to vast amounts of information locally and globally in different time zones and geographical places. The *speed* and *automation* of ICT allow tasks of storing, transforming and displaying information to be carried out by the technologies, enabling users to read, observe, interrogate, interpret, analyse and synthesise information at higher levels. *Quality* can be recognised in the potential to present and publish work to a high standard of appearance and reproduction. *Multimodality* is reflected in the interaction between modes of text, image, sound, hypertextuality and non-linearity. Issues of *neutrality* and *social credibility* open a variety of debates about the impact of ICT on our social and cultural lives.

What can ICT offer that other tools cannot?

A characteristic of creativity with digital technologies is the way features of ICT can be experimented with and exploited to support creative processes. Learners and teachers, therefore, need to have a range of experiences in which they can engage, play and become familiar with the distinctive contributions that ICT can make to their creative practices which other media and tools may not offer.

ICT capability is more than competence with a set of skills and techniques with particular digital technologies, but encompasses such skills being turned to meaningful use. It can be described as an ability which is used actively, involving understanding, informed choice, critical evaluation and being open, or susceptible, to development (Loveless 2003). The view of ICT capability found in the National Curriculum for England focuses on the purpose of activities which can be carried out right across the curriculum, not restricted to specific subject areas. There are five main 'strands' in the Primary and Secondary ICT curriculum for Key Stages 1–4:

1   finding things out

2   developing ideas and making things happen

3   exchanging and sharing information; reviewing

4   modifying and evaluating work as it progresses

5   breadth of study in which pupils are taught the knowledge, skills and understanding.

These 'strands' are sometimes difficult to separate as they weave around and into each other. A closer examination of the language used in the ICT National Curriculum indicates that much of it reflects the processes, not only of skill and technique, but also of higher-order thinking which is an important component of creativity (Higgins 2001; Wegerif 2002). For example:

■ *Synthesis* – create, compose, invent, hypothesise, what would happen if . . .?, design, be original, combine from several sources;

■ *Analysis* – categorise, compare/contrast, alike/different, cause/effect, relevant/irrelevant, find fallacies, fact/opinion;

■ *Evaluation* – give an opinion, judge, rate – best/worst, choose, recommend, what to do differently.

Interaction between the features of ICT, ICT capability and creativity

There is potential for interaction between the features of ICT, ICT capability and creativity. ICT capability draws upon the features of ICT in order to develop experiences and expertise in the strands of the ICT National Curriculum. These, in turn, interact with the characteristics of creativity and contribute to the processes within a range of different subjects that also provide relevant and authentic contexts for the development of ICT capability. For example, children using a web-design package such as 'SiteCentral' to develop a website about Victorian Britain will certainly need to develop their ICT capability. The software, combined with ICT capability, provides the potential for creativity, particularly in provisionality and multi-modality that enable children to experiment with different juxtapositions of text, image and sound, but they might not use this, preferring instead to reproduce what they find in textbooks. One way to prepare this activity might be to get the children, working in small groups, to say what they like and do not like about a range of very different websites before generating a few alternative ideas for their own website. It is not access to ICT that 'delivers' creativity but the opportunities such access can afford, when structured by teachers, for interaction, participation and the active demonstration of imagination, production, purpose, originality and value.

Using ICT in the creative classroom

Creative processes in the use of ICT can support the development of imagination, problem-solving, risk-taking and divergent thinking. These processes, which describe pupils' creative thinking and behaviour, can be summarised as:

- questioning and challenging;
- making connections and seeing relationships;
- envisaging what might be;
- playing with ideas;
- representing ideas; and
- evaluating the effects of ideas.

Creativity can be seen in the interaction between a person's thoughts and actions, their knowledge and skills within a subject 'domain', and a social and cultural context which can encourage, evaluate and reward. This has important implications for thinking about creativity and learning, where the context could be a school classroom or learning environment that can either nurture or dismiss the development of creative individuals, groups and communities.

This interaction can be seen in the framework for creativity presented by the National Advisory Committee on Creative and Cultural Education (NACCCE 1999). In this report creativity is defined as: 'imaginative activity fashioned so as to produce outcomes that are both original and of value'.

Personal and community characteristics can be expressed in approaches *to using imagination, the fashioning process and pursuing purpose*. These processes also draw upon knowledge, concepts and skills within learning domains which provide conceptual tools and ways of working in fashioning and pursuing purpose. The levels of achievement of *originality* for individuals, peer groups or within the domain are evaluated within the social and cultural context, while the *judgement of value* can relate to critical reflection for the individual as well as recognition of a unique contribution to the domain itself (ibid.).

ICT and creativity in the curriculum

Creative activities with new technologies include developing ideas, making connections, creating and making, collaboration, communication and evaluation. The following sections present examples of such activities which illustrate how children are able to use ICT not only to demonstrate elements of the ICT National Curriculum, but also to support and enhance a broader creative framework within the subject context.

What would happen if . . .?

The ICT strand of 'Developing ideas and making things happen' is often associated with the use of digital technology to explore the question 'What would happen if . . .? Software to support this includes simulations for modelling, spreadsheets or control technology to sense, monitor, measure and control sequences of events mediated by devices such as programmable toys or to control software applications. Versions of these applications have been used in mathematics and Design & Technology for nearly twenty years, but more recently the early stages of the development of ideas and design have been supported by software that enables brainstorming and collaboration through concept mapping (e.g. *Inspiration*) and multimedia authoring (e.g. *HyperStudio*).

Web-based resources

Web-based resources are also available for children to explore and test ideas on-line. Resources such as the Tracy Beaker web pages on the BBC Schools website (http://www.bbc.co.uk/cbbc/tracybeaker/) or the Sodaplay site which enables children to construct and animate models on screen (http://www.sodaplay.com/) are examples of the provisionality, interactivity and range of ICT which can underpin playful approaches to trying out imaginative ideas.

Digital image manipulation

Dave Simpson describes the ways in which digital cameras and image manipulation software can be used in exploration and improvisation 'within' drama activities rather than just to record final outcomes. He works with groups using digital images in the 'sketching' stages of the exploration and interpretation of texts, such as the multi-layered illustrated children's book *Not Now, Bernard*. These are then developed as an integral element of the drama as children respond to their constructed, manipulated images and incorporate them into their developing improvisations (Simpson 1999, 2001).

Making connections

Finding things out in order to support, challenge, inform and develop ideas is an important element in the processes of using imagination, fashioning and pursuing purpose. ICT can play a role in making connections with other people, projects, information and resources through the internet, World Wide Web and CD-ROM, and the use of these communications technologies is well documented (e.g. the Teaching Ideas website focuses on the use of the internet with children and teachers – http://www.teachingideas.co.uk/welcome). The EarlyBirds Music is an example of a website that provides multimedia examples of video, sound and links to music resources for early, primary and special education (http://www.earlybirdsmusic.com). Access to worldwide galleries and museums can provide resources for stimulation and research. Access to practitioners, such as artists, designers, engineers and architects, through email or video-conferencing can establish networks and communities sharing expertise, questions and work in progress. The Museum Open Learning Initiatives (MOLLI) is an example of such a 'window' to artefacts, activities and work produced by children and adults in the community in response to particular exhibitions and to individual artists' work (http://www.molli.org.uk).

Creating and making meaning

The weaving of imagination, fashioning, pursuing purposes and being original needs to move beyond the use of tools and techniques for their own sake in the creation, drafting, editing and refining processes. Creating tangible outcomes, such as an image, a poem, a drama, a 3D construction or a movie involves not only the physical act of making, but also an ongoing 'dialogue' where 'the maker produces and the work responds'. The artist Terry Taylor places this dialogue at the centre of his work with children and digital images:

> It is the representation of meaning that is the key that elevates production to a position beyond the merely decorative ... By dialogue I mean the dynamic and creative cognitive processes involved when encoding and decoding meaning in visual texts ... This takes time and a continuation of intention and cannot be achieved by ad hoc projects based on mechanical processes.

> (Loveless and Taylor 2000: 65)

The work of artists like Terry can be seen in school projects where children work with visual artists using different media, including the digital technologies of scanners, cameras and graphics software. The children produce pieces in response to a variety of stimuli from the artist, who then encourages them to display and evaluate each other's work in progress as well as final outcomes, and to share the discoveries they had made in the techniques with different media and tools. Digital images need not always be the final products, but can sometimes act as stimuli or sketches for development of representations in other media.

Technology can play a distinctive role in these activities by providing opportunities for the children to capture, edit and transform digital data in order to make meanings. The creative processes of imagination, fashioning and 'flow' are supported by the immediacy of the presentation, the ease of manipulation and the possibilities of 'leaving a trail' of work in progress in order to trace the development of ideas. These characteristics of ICT are now also being exploited in software applications which are accessible for young learners for the creative production of moving images with digital video (e.g. *iMovie*), music (e.g. *Dance eJay*), multimedia texts (e.g. *Hyperstudio*, *Textease 2000*) and the creation of 3D virtual worlds (e.g. *ActiveWorlds*).

Collaboration

Our understanding of how we learn has developed through recognition of the social and situated nature in which knowledge is constructed during interaction and communication with others in communities (Bruner 1996). The speed and range of communications technology, such as email, video-conferencing and mobile communications, enable children to collaborate with others in immediate and dynamic ways during their creative work in progress. Collaboration with artists, writers and fictional characters in 'non-residence' through email or video-conferences offers children opportunities to work with others to generate ideas, pursue purpose and evaluate ongoing, original work. Children participating in the Interactive Education Project focused on the use of email to explore how awareness of audience and purpose shapes writing by corresponding with two 'Viking settlers' (Sutherland *et al.* 2002). The Bristol Internet Project enabled children in schools in two different communities in the city to collaborate with each other on making visual images over time and distance. They used digital cameras and 'paint' programs to construct images of themselves doing various activities, from playing basketball to flying. These images were attached to email messages to their 'key pals' in the other school, asking questions such as 'Who am I?' and 'What am I doing?' Artists in each school worked with the children to interpret, respond to and manipulate the images received before sending them back with their ideas developed further (Loveless and Taylor 2000). The creative focus of this work is on the children's development of their imaginative ideas, the use of a variety of tools and media and the opportunities for evaluation and critique with peers.

In these examples of collaboration we can see how the distinctive features of ICT mentioned earlier support creativity, particularly provisionality and interactivity. A slightly different but compatible approach to developing creativity with ICT activities is to focus on developing the creative properties of the collaboration itself. Some conversations around or through computers are more creative than others. By preparing children and young people to work together with computers, teachers can have a big impact on the quality of their collaboration (Wegerif and Dawes 2004). Creativity seems to thrive in dialogues that are based on warmth and trust so that new things can be said that support the development of a joint product that meets shared standards of quality. Such creative conversations – conversations that are at the same time stimulating, supportive and challenging – can be encouraged through the establishing of shared ground rules. The sort of ground rules that help creative conversations are:

- listening carefully;
- offering encouragement to others to develop their ideas;
- building on the words of others;
- using open questions; and
- allowing pauses for creative thought.

While such creative conversations can be held through computers, via the internet, as we have seen in the examples above, there is plenty of evidence that they can also be stimulated and supported in pairs or by small groups of children using simple software running on stand-alone computers. The computer screen serves as an excellent focus for collaborations and the single entry through keyboard or mouse can mean, with the right guidance, that children or young people have to work together.

Joint creativity is very clear in one example, first presented by Mercer in 1995, in which two ten-year-old girls, Katie and Anne, were working on the production of their own class newspaper, using some desktop publishing software for schools called *Front Page Extra*. At the point the sequence begins, they have been engaged in the task for about an hour and a quarter and are trying to compose some text for their front page.

Fantabuloso (from Mercer 1995:101, lightly edited)

Katie: Okay, so right then. What shall we write?

Anne: We can have something like those autograph columns and things like that and items, messages.

Katie: Inside these covers [*pause for 3 secs*] our fun filled . . .

Anne: That's it!

Katie: Yeah.

Anne: Inside these fabulous fun-filled covers are . . . how can we have a fun-filled cover? Let me try.

Katie: Inside these [*pause for 3-plus secs*]
Hah, huh [*both laugh*]

Anne: You sound happy on this. Fantabuloso! [*laugh*]

Katie: Inside these fant . . ., inside these fun-filled . . . no, inside these covers, these fantastic, these brilliant . . .

Anne: Brilliant!

Katie: Is it brilliant?

Anne: No.

Katie: No. Fantast . . . fantabuloso, shall we put that?

Anne: Yeah [*inaudible*] fantabluloso.

Katie: Fan-tab-u-lo-so.

Anne: . . . loso. Fantabuloso.

Katie: Fantabuloso . . . oso.

In this extract it is possible to see how creative conversations work. The girls are obviously motivated and stimulated by working together and building on each other's words. They are playing, but they are also serious in their effort to do the creative task set by the teacher. They could almost be a couple of creative marketing executives trying to find a new name for a product. Products with very similar names to the word 'Fantabuloso' that they create together: Fab, Fanta, Brillo etc., already exist and were presumably thought up through a similar kind of conversation. At the same time as generating original ideas they work together to fashion these ideas and they apply judgements of value to select the preferred response. Katie asks 'Is it *brilliant*?', i.e. Does this word fit?, and she agrees with Anna that it is not quite right. Both then converge on 'fantabuloso'.

Similar kinds of creative collaborations can occur around almost any kind of software. The teacher's role is crucial in creating and maintaining a climate in the classroom in which such creative conversations can occur. In particular, it helps to establish ground rules for talking with the class, ground rules such as listening to each other, asking open questions and building on each other's ideas.

Conclusion

This chapter has argued that there can be a positive interaction between creativity, ICT capability and the features of digital technologies that offer learners and teachers opportunities to work in new and different ways. The activities described have been designed not to promote ICT skills in themselves, but to use ICT resources in developing children's creative experiences and expression. The activities focus on the creative processes used in developing imaginative ideas, making meaning, sharing work in progress and evaluating outcomes. Teachers play an important role in designing and planning stimulating environments that offer a variety of experiences, tools, techniques and media that support and challenge children's creative imagination, engagement, motivation, skill, application and judgement. Teachers can also create and sustain a climate of creativity in their classrooms through establishing ground rules for collaboration with and around ICT that foster shared creativity.

Acknowledgement

Some of the ideas behind this chapter are developed further in Loveless, A. (2003) 'Creating spaces in the primary curriculum: ICT in creative subjects'. *The Curriculum Journal*, 14(1), Spring, 5–21.

Notes

1   Founder of ZeroOne, a non-profit-making art and technology organisation (see http://www.groundzero.org/).

2   Winners had the chance to travel to Japan, the home of RoboFesta International, to build the robots that they had designed. Many children were inspired by this challenge to exercise their creativity. Over 32,000 designs were submitted. The RoboFesta UK team hopes to make all of these designs available on its website (http://robofesta.open.ac.uk/ see Johnson *et al.* 2002). In the guidelines to the competition the children were instructed to say what their robot does (specification) and how it does it (analysis). They were also encouraged to come up with designs 'that could really work' (evaluation).

Further reading

Bruner, J. (1996) *The Culture of Education*. Cambridge, MA: Harvard University Press.

Higgins, C. (2001) 'Information and Communication Technology' in D. Eyre and L. McClure *Curriculum Provision for the Gifted and Talented in the Primary School*. London: David Fulton.

Johnson, J., Hirst, A. and Garner, S. (2002) 'Learning from designing the RoboFesta – Blue Peter Robots', AROB-7. Proceedings of the International Symposium on Artificial Life and Robotics (ed. M. Sugisaka and H. Tanaka) (ISBN 4-9900462-2-6), Oita University.

Loveless, A. M. (1997) 'Visual literacy and new technology in primary schools: the Glebe School Project'. *Journal of Computing and Childhood Education*, 8(2/3), 98–110.

Loveless, A. (2003) *The Role of ICT*. London: Continuum.

Loveless, A. and Taylor, T. (2000) 'Creativity, Visual Literacy and ICT', in M. Leask and J. Meadows *Teaching and Learning with ICT in the Primary School*. London: Routledge, 65–80.

Mercer, N. (1995) *The Guided Construction of Knowledge: Talk amongst Teachers and Learners*. Clevedon: Multilingual Matters.

NACCCE (1999) *All Our Futures: Creativity, Culture and Education*. National Advisory Committee on Creative and Cultural Education: London: DfEE and DCMS.

Simpson, D. (1999) 'The making of drama? Working on a children's novel with a digital camera'. *Drama Magazine*, Winter.

Simpson, D. (2001) 'Not now technology? Exploring David McKee's "Not Now, Bernard" '. *Drama Magazine*, Summer.

Sutherland, R., Breeze, N., Gall, M., Godwin, S., Matthewman, S., Shortis, T. and Triggs, P. (2002) *Pedagogy and Purpose for ICT in Primary Education: Learning with Technologies in School, Home and Community*. Manchester: International Federation for Information Processing Working Group 3.5 on Informatics and Elementary Education.

Wegerif, R. (2002) *Thinking skills, technology and learning: A Review of the Literature for NESTA* FutureLab (www.nestafuturelab.org) ISBN 0-9544695-2-6.

Wegerif, R. and Dawes, L. (2004) *Thinking and Learning with ICT: Raising Achievement in Primary Classrooms*. London: Routledge.

Creative design and technology

David Barlex

'Quantum Tunnelling Composite (QTC) is clever stuff. It comes as thin sheets or a powder. It can be built into textiles or fixed to hard surfaces. In a relaxed state it is a good insulator. When it is stretched, squashed or twisted it becomes a conductor. The harder you stretch, squash or twist it the better it conducts. It's already been used in power tools and a robot hand. What would you use it for?'

THIS CHAPTER IS IN five parts. Part 1 is a discussion of the relationship between designing and creativity and a brief summary of the findings of a QCA/Nuffield Curriculum Centre seminar, which developed a model for the conditions needed for creativity in the design and technology classroom. Part 2 describes the work of children at Key Stage 2 in designing and making picture-frames that stand up unaided and display images of favourite people. Part 3 describes the work of children at Key Stage 3 in designing and making automata and simple food products. Part 4 describes what happens when children aged 14 (Year 9) are encouraged to design in groups in the knowledge that what they design they will *not* have to make. Part 5 presents a summary and discussion.

Creativity and designing

The NACCCE report *All Our Futures: Creativity, Culture and Education* (Department for Education and Employment 1999) contends that a national strategy for creative and cultural education is essential to unlock the potential of every young person. The report argues that creativity is a process, not an event, involving a complex combination of controlled and non-controlled elements, unconscious as well as conscious mental processes, non-directed as well as directed thought, intuitive as well as rational calculation. It claims that deferment of judgement is invaluable; that at the right time, in the right way, critical appraisal is essential. At the wrong point, criticism and the cold hand of realism can kill an emerging idea. In their view, creativity involves two modes of thought – generative and evaluative – and they claim it is unlikely that a finished piece will be produced in one move. It defined creativity as 'imaginative activity fashioned so as to produce outcomes that are both original and of value' (p. 29), and so saw creativity in terms of the task in hand as having four features:

- using imagination;
- pursuing purposes;
- being original; and
- being of value.

The exact nature of these features will vary from subject to subject according to the purposes of creativity within particular subjects. In design and technology the creative process is related very strongly to the act of designing. Buchanan (1996 : 17) argues, 'the problem for designers is to conceive and plan what does not yet exist'. This is echoed by Ropohl (1997: 69), who notes that 'the designer has to determine spatial and temporal details, which cannot yet be observed'. This activity is complex. As Cross *et al.* (1986: 29) note:

> a designer attends simultaneously to many levels of detail as he designs. The level of attention encompasses the range of design considerations from overall concept to small particulars. Many of the small particulars only surface to be dealt with consciously when they become critical.

Design tasks are 'open' or 'wicked' tasks. They are not merely ill-defined and multi-dimensional but also individual, have no stopping rules, and are capable of multiple solutions (Rittel, quoted in Churchman 1967). Cross (2002) has considered the nature of designing in two ways. From a brief review of designers on designing he clarifies what designers do:

- produce novel, unexpected solutions;
- tolerate uncertainty, working with incomplete information;
- apply imagination and constructive forethought to practical problems;
- use drawings and other modelling media as a means of problem solving.

(p. 127)

From a review of studies of designing he summarises the core features of design ability as compromising the ability to:

- resolve ill-defined problems;
- adopt solution-focusing strategies;
- employ abductive/productive/appositional thinking; and
- use non-verbal, graphic/spatial modelling media.

(p. 131)

To ensure that the act of designing can be seen as a creative act in educational terms it is important to ask 'Do these descriptions of activity and design ability correspond to the view of creativity as expressed in the NACCCE report *All Our Futures: Creativity, Culture and Education* (Department for Education and Employment, 1999) i.e. using imagination, pursuing purposes, being original and being of value?'

Producing novel, unexpected solutions can be seen to correspond to being original. Applying imagination and constructive forethought to practical problems can be seen to correspond to both using imagination and being of value. Using drawings and other modelling media as a means of problem solving can be seen to correspond to pursuing a purpose. Resolving ill-defined problems can be seen to correspond to pursuing a purpose. Adopting solution-focusing strategies can be seen to correspond to being concerned with value. Employing abductive / productive / appositional thinking can be seen to correspond to using imagination. Using non-verbal, graphic/spatial modelling media can be seen to correspond to being imaginative and original.

This brief analysis shows clearly that design activity and design abilities match the view of creativity as expressed in the report *All Our Futures: Creativity, Culture and Education* (Department for Education and Employment 1999). Given the revision of the Orders for design and technology in the National Curriculum to include specific mention of creativity, and the correspondence of designing to creative activity as described by Cross (2002), there is no reason to assume that designing within design & technology should not be a creative activity. However, while it is likely that the activities of professional designers as described by Cross will be creative, this begs the question as to the classroom conditions that will enable children, who are novice designers, to design in a creative way. To address this question QCA and the Nuffield Curriculum Centre invited 20 teachers to attend a full-day meeting at which they presented pupils' work in art & design and design & technology. This was followed by visits to a selection of schools to watch lessons in progress and a further full-day meeting in which teachers presented and discussed pupils' work.

From this overview it was possible to identify four features that had to be in place for pupils to act creatively in either subject:

1   The activity had to be presented in a context to which the pupils could relate.

2   The activity had to be supported by a significant stimulus which was often, but not exclusively, intensely visual.

3   Focused teaching was necessary to provide knowledge, understanding and skills.

4   An attitude of continuous reflection needed to be encouraged.

But an analysis of the work revealed that these four features alone do not ensure creative activity. The deciding factor is the way they are managed. This must be done so that pupils can *handle uncertainty in exploring and developing outcomes*. There must be some risk associated with the endeavour in terms of the 'originality' of the activity as far

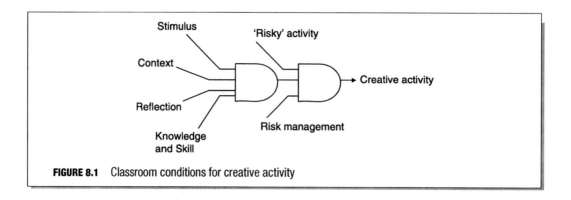

FIGURE 8.1 Classroom conditions for creative activity

as the individual pupil is concerned. If the outcome is certain to be successful, all possibility of 'failure' is eliminated; if there are no 'butterflies in the tummy' at some stage in the endeavour then the outcome will be mundane. This is illustrated in Figure 8.1. The diagram describes the necessary, but not sufficient conditions required for creativity (stimulus, context, reflection, knowledge and skill) as inputs into a four-input AND gate. There is an output when all four inputs take place but this output will not lead to creative activity unless it takes place in a situation in which 'risky' activity is possible, and where this risk is managed. Hence these three conditions become inputs into a triple AND gate, which gives an output of creative activity, providing all three inputs take place simultaneously.

The instrument of children's creativity in design & technology is the designing and making assignment (DMA). In these assignments children are expected to generate and develop design ideas and then make a prototype product based on those design ideas which can be evaluated against the performance criteria the design was intended to meet. In dealing with novice designers (children in school) teachers orchestrate the number and complexity of the design decisions that the children have to make in carrying out a designing and making activity, in order to ensure that the assignment is appropriately challenging without being daunting, and requires pupils to use particular parts of the design & technology programme of study. So an important first step in getting a view of the creativity that can be exhibited by pupils in tackling a particular DMA is to audit the range of design decisions that are likely to be made by pupils tackling the assignment. This audit can be carried out using five key areas of design decision: conceptual (overall purpose of the design, the sort of product that it will be); technical (how the design will work); aesthetic (what the design will look like); constructional (how the design will be put together); and marketing (who the design is for, where it will be used, how it will be sold). This can be represented visually as shown in Figure 8.2, with each feature at a corner of a pentagon and each area of design decision connected to each other area. This interconnectedness is an important feature of design decisions. A change of decision within one area will affect some, if not all, of the design decisions that are made within the others. For example, if the way a design is to work

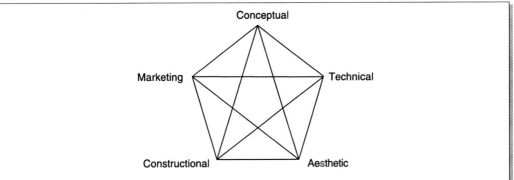

FIGURE 8.2 One way of representing the areas of design decision that pupils may need to make when tackling a DMA

is changed, this will almost certainly affect what the design looks like and how it is constructed. It may also have far-reaching effects in changing some of the purposes that the design can meet and who might be able to use it.

Usually the teacher identifies the sort of product the children will be designing and making. This makes it very difficult for children to engage in conceptual design. This issue will be dealt with later in Part 4 on designing without making. Even if the type of product is identified for the pupils there are still many opportunities for making design decisions in the other areas. Consider the designing and making of a puppet theatre and puppets. The pupils can make decisions about who will use the puppets and what for (marketing decisions), what sort of puppets would be appropriate, the sort of theatre such puppets would need, the nature of props and scenery plus any special effects that might accompany the performance. These decisions will encompass a host of technical, aesthetic and constructional design decisions.

In looking at the products designed and made by a class of pupils it will be important to look for differences and similarities in the work produced as this will give insight into the features of creative activity: the levels of imagination; the extent of originality; the variety of value in the different offerings; and the differing purposes pursued. The examples described in the next two parts will be considered in terms of the way the teacher met the conditions for creative activity, the difference and similarity of the work produced and how this is related to design decisions.

Designing by children in design & technology at Key Stage 2

Creativity through designing and making a picture-frame

Before the work began the teacher had asked the children to bring in from home images and other items associated with a favourite person. The resulting favourite people covered a wide range – football players, cartoon characters, film and book characters. The class discussed these briefly and the teacher established that none of the items was so precious that it could not be cut up or glued into position onto a card frame. All of the images were from easily obtainable popular magazines so this was not a problem.

The teacher drew attention to the photo-frame display she had prepared and also showed the class a mask through which pictures could be seen. She then asked the children to draw the mask that they would use to show pictures of their favourite person. The children had little difficulty in complying with this request using a variety of different shaped windows arranged in different ways.

Then the teacher introduced the problem of the frame falling over. What could be done to stop this? The initial responses included *papier maché* and crinkly paper. The teacher suggested that these might make the frame look more attractive but questioned whether they would help it stand up. Then a pupil suggested they could add another piece of card. The teacher said that this might work, but to find out exactly how to do it they would need to investigate. She gave each pupil some card and scissors and asked them to make different ways of getting the card to stand up straight. Most pupils generated a single idea to which they became very attached. One pupil developed four different solutions but she was the exception. The teacher introduced the idea of a simple blowing test to check whether the proposed structure was actually stable. The teacher collected together the work and used a question-and-answer session with the class to identify the different sorts of structures that they had developed and to discuss which ones worked well and which did not.

Several problems emerged from this investigation. Simple solutions can be achieved by merely folding the card. Thin pieces of additional card can be used as props; but there are problems when these are not stiff enough. The situation can be improved by adding a tie between the base of the frame and the base of the prop. The point of attachment of the prop is important. If it is too low the card of the frame flops backwards causing the whole to fall over. The need for careful scoring before attachment of card to be used as props or ties needs to be emphasised and will need practising by some pupils.

The teacher explained to the class that cutting out the masks they needed to act as windows for their pictures might be tricky so it would be a good idea to practise cutting out the shapes they needed. It was indeed the case that many children found this difficult. They had lots of previous experience of cutting out around the outside of a shape but cutting around the inside of a shape to leave a hole was much more difficult. Starting off is particularly tricky and they tried the technique of 'stabbing' with a pencil onto the place where the cut would begin, the underside being supported by a blob of blu-tack. The typically round-ended primary classroom scissors did not lend themselves to penetrating the small hole. In many cases the teacher and classroom assistant had to start them off, but even then some children produced a cut that was uneven – a series of short jagged cuts. Small circles proved particularly tricky.

Now the teacher set the class the task of producing the finished photo-frames. Despite the best efforts of the teacher and the classroom assistant to get pupils to reconsider their approach to making the photo-frame stable a significant number of children insisted on staying with their first idea for making the frame stand up, although the blow test showed that it was not as effective as it might be and that there were other solutions available.

The teacher had organised the teaching so that the conditions for creativity were to a large extent met. She had provided a context to which the children could relate (celebrating a favourite person). She had provided stimulus with the display of photo-frames. She had developed appropriate knowledge and skills through small tasks (developing the mask, exploring ways to achieve stability) and throughout she had encouraged reflection. The children were encouraged to take 'sensible' risks in using their learning to develop a stable structure although both the teacher and the classroom assistant noted many children's reluctance to move from their first idea. They decided that this was probably because they were only rarely given the chance to see a range of ideas at the development stage. This led them to suggest that in future this should become a feature of the way they taught design and technology as current practice was leading to a lack of openness to ideas and critical thinking. The risk management was handled by providing individual support as needed. There were clearly opportunities for the children to make a wide range of design decisions – technical (how the frame would be made stable); aesthetic (how the picture(s) would be displayed); constructional (exactly how the different elements would be joined together). The work across the class showed several different approaches to the problem of creating a self-standing frame. No two frames looked alike although several adopted similar solutions. All were individual in that they displayed the particular favourite of the child concerned.

Designing by pupils in design and technology at Key Stage 3

Creativity through designing and making automata

Designing and making a simple cam toy

Here the teacher set up a situation in which pupils in Year 7 designed and made simple cam toys. He allowed no conceptual design decisions, the pupils were told they would design and make a mechanical toy. He limited the technical design decisions by restricting them to the use of cams and simple friction drives. The toy only had to appeal to the pupil doing the designing and making so there was little in the way of marketing design decisions. He gave very clear instructions as to the construction of the frame to support the drive mechanism (a cam/friction drive shaft) so there were only a few opportunities for constructional design decisions in the mechanism – exactly where to drill the holes to take the cam followers, for example. He allowed moderate aesthetic design decisions in that the pupils could choose any animal to be the 'toy', but he restricted the materials from which they could make the animal form to wooden strip and dowel. Developing recognisable animal forms from this limited repertoire required an interesting combination of aesthetic and constructional decisions. He allowed a wide range of paint to be used for decoration. The teacher had organised the teaching so that the conditions for creativity were to some extent met. The context setting was limited. He relied on the class's previous experience of success in designing and making with him to provide motivation. The main stimulus was his enthusiasm for them to be successful and his high expectation of careful construction. He successfully taught the limited knowledge and skill he thought they needed to be successful in their designing and making. He enabled reflection through conversations with individual pupils when they were constructing the basic frame and deciding which animal and movements to choose. He limited the risk-taking quite severely and this manifests itself in the similarity of the outcomes. He argued for this limitation on design decisions on the grounds that the pupils lacked both the technical and constructional experience to be given wider choice *and that* within this limited range there was plenty of opportunity for the pupils to be creative at levels commensurate with both their ability and imagination.

As pupils get older and acquire more knowledge and skill the range of design decisions they can make should become wider, and in this respect their creativity might manifest itself more obviously in the differences between the products of individual pupils. So we should ask what differences there might be in the teaching approach of a mechanical toy project for pupils in Year 9 who should be capable of a more sophisticated response than pupils in Year 7. In this case the teacher set up the situation by teaching the class about a range of different mechanisms. She did this first by introducing them to a range of already constructed mechanisms made from the Fisher Technic Construction Kit. Working in pairs, pupils explored what each of the mechanisms did in terms of input movement and output movement. Then the teacher set a challenge. She asked each pair to choose their favourite mechanism and to make a working copy of this from MDF, dowel and appropriate mechanical components. This taught all sorts of 'tacit' understanding about mechanisms – alignment, tolerances and clearances. With a little direction the class of pupils working in pairs produced a reference set of 'made' mechanisms as opposed to 'kit' mechanisms and there were pairs of pupils who could act as experts on any one of these mechanisms. This bridged the gap between kit work – designed to be stripped down and put back in the box – and the prototyping required to produce a finished and working mechanical product.

The brief for the DMA was to design and make a mechanical toy that will provide amusement and intrigue and which will be sold in a large pet shop. The toy should use just one mechanism and look like an animal. Pupils were still unable to engage with conceptual designing as the given brief was quite closed. The marketing decisions had, to a large extent, been made for the pupils but there were considerable opportunities for technical, aesthetic and constructional design decisions. There was a much greater variety in the response of the Year 9 pupils compared with that of the Year 7 pupils.

The teacher had organised the teaching so that the conditions for creativity were largely met. As in the work with the Year 7 pupils the stimulus was limited (although the pupils found the preliminary exploration of mechanisms intriguing and motivating) but the work was placed in a context that made sense – a pet shop exhibiting moving toy animals. The teaching of appropriate knowledge and skill was accomplished in an innovative way that encouraged the pupils to reflect on what they and others had learned and how this could be used in their designing and making. In deciding on the animal form, the movement it would make and the mechanism to achieve this, the pupils were taking risks, but these were informed risks, managed to some extent by their immediate previous experience with mechanisms and discussion with the teacher about the feasibility of their ideas.

The difference between the work of the Year 7 and the Year 9 pupils is clear and illustrates the importance of the teacher restricting the design decisions that the pupils make *and* supporting them in making those design decisions both *before* and *during* the DMA. Support before the DMA involved the teaching of specific knowledge and skills – an understanding of several different mechanisms and how they might be constructed in the case of the Year 9 pupils, and an understanding of just two similar mechanisms and how to construct them in the case of the Year 7 pupils. Support during the DMA required the teacher to engage the pupils in conversations through which they articulated and justified their design decisions and could be challenged to be more or less creative depending on the teacher's perception of their ability to be successful in carrying through those decisions to completion.

Comparison with the work at Key Stage 2 raises an interesting issue. The work from Year 7 is less individualistic because those pupils were given less scope for their creativity than the pupils in Year 4.

Creativity through designing and making simple food products

The following example is taken from the Revised Nuffield Secondary Design and Technology Project materials (Barlex *et al.* 2000). The pupils have to design and make a range of food products in response to the theme 'The Healthy Heart'. This task was developed by Marion Rutland at Roehampton University of Surrey. Having completed some focused practical tasks to teach specific making and evaluation skills, the pupils are given access to a range of starter recipes and told to choose one to modify so that it meets the criteria of the British Heart Foundation for food that is 'healthy for your heart':

> 10g sugar per 100g product
> 20g fat per 100g product
> 5g saturated fat per 100g product
> 3g fibre per 100g product
> 0.5g sodium per 100g product

Here the pupils' attention is focused on the amounts of particular ingredients within a recipe and how they might adjust these. The exact consequences of any adjustments in terms of flavour, odour, texture and appearance are not certain until they have been made and the resultant product observed and tasted. It is possible and sometimes necessary for the pupils to enact several iterations before they obtain a product that is tasty as well as healthy.

The pupils make no conceptual design decisions; the teacher has decided on a range of existing products for modification, no new types of products were being envisaged. The main marketing decision – food products for those wanting to eat healthily – has already been made. Marketing to particular groups could be achieved by different packaging according to the group pupils wished to attract, but that is a graphic design exercise and was outside the scope of this piece of work. There is an interaction of the technical, constructional and aesthetic design decisions.

Asparagus and cheese quiche

The pupil made the following changes:

200g plain flour to 100g plain flour plus 100g wholemeal flour to increase fibre;

semi-skimmed milk instead of plain milk to reduce fat content;

asparagus instead of bacon (as in a classic quiche recipe) to reduce fat and add fibre;

low-fat cheese instead of ordinary cheese to reduce fat.

Courgette and tomato soup

Starting with a cream of mushroom soup recipe the pupil made the following changes:

courgettes and tomatoes instead of mushrooms to increase fibre and vitamins;

margarine instead of butter to reduce saturated fat;

water instead of milk and stock to reduce fat and sodium.

Here the teacher set a context that would appeal to Key Stage 3 pupils – healthy eating amidst current concerns about the effect of diet on health – and provided a stimulus through the British Heart Foundation materials. He taught appropriate knowledge and skills through a set of preliminary tasks that taught the pupils food-handling techniques and nutritional content of different sorts of food ingredients. He encouraged reflection through discussion of nutritional modification and resultant sensory differences and the need for different food-handling techniques. The risk taken by the pupils was in choosing nutritional modification without the experience to know in advance the sensory consequences. However, given the short time it takes to try out and evaluate any one modification, this is not a problem and the teacher could manage this by simply maintaining efficient food-handling techniques. This activity is not as creative as developing a completely new type of food product or a new recipe. However, most people, including those who have cooking as a major leisure time activity, never develop a completely new recipe but adapt recipes to produce food products for particular purposes.

Sometimes these might be aesthetic. (I can remember spending a long time with my youngest son, helping him decorate a Batman birthday cake for his elder brother.) Sometimes they can be economic (related to marketing) in that there is a limited budget for ingredients. Sometimes they are constructional – we have to be able to cook this in a microwave oven. Sometimes they are technical, as in the cases above, to meet dietary requirements. The role of the teacher in developing creativity through food technology is to provide pupils with the knowledge, understanding and skill that will enable them to make ever more sophisticated recipe modifications.

Creativity through designing without making

This section of the chapter draws on the work of the Young Foresight Project. It operates in Year 9 of the design & technology curriculum in England. A key feature of the project is that pupils work in groups to design, but do *not* make, products and services for the future, taking new and emerging technologies as their starting point. The project has produced a short stimulus video about a new material, quantum tunnelling composite (QTC), which has considerable technological potential. The video is used as the starting point for a Young Foresight challenge, which can be summarised as follows:

> Quantum Tunnelling Composite (QTC) is clever stuff. It comes as thin sheets or a powder. It can be built into textiles or fixed to hard surfaces. In a relaxed state it is a good insulator. When it is stretched, squashed or twisted it becomes a conductor. The harder you stretch, squash or twist it the better it conducts. It's already been used in power tools and a robot hand. What would you use it for?

Two examples of pupils' work are described and discussed. The first is a design idea produced by the pupil and then as a development of this drawing carried out by Kursty Groves, an experienced product designer, from Pankhurst Design & Development Ltd. It is a child's toothbrush, which uses QTC to detect whether children are brushing their teeth properly and rewards them by playing a tune if they are. The second is a device to be worn by a person who suffers from epilepsy. The QTC detects the attack through the rapid expansion and contraction of the jaw muscles and relays this information via blue-tooth technology to a transmitter worn on the belt. The transmitter sends a signal to a global positioning satellite, which relays the wearer's position to the nearest hospital summoning medical aid. In addition, the transmitter broadcasts a sound message to passers-by apologising for any inconvenience and asking them to place the person having the attack on their side with their tongue pulled out to avoid choking.

In both cases the pupils have made marketing decisions in that they have identified who will use the product that they design. In both cases they have made conceptual decisions in that they have conceived the nature of the product that they will design. They have made limited technical decisions in that, while they have started with a given technology, they have added other technologies to it in order to achieve their desired outcome – logic circuits and a music-making chip in the case of the toothbrush; blue-tooth, satellite communications and a sound chip in the case of the epilepsy aid. Their original drawings show some aesthetic design decisions and these have been built upon by those illustrating the concepts further. They have made no construction decisions as this was not part of their remit.

The context of this activity is one that appeals to pupils – their future world. The stimulus is provided by the introductory TV programme. The knowledge and skills required for the creative activity were provided by a set of prior small tasks designed specifically to support designing to meet needs and wants. The reflective activity needed to generate, develop and communicate design ideas that are novel is provided by the collaborative group-work situation in which peer group review is an essential ingredient. The 'risky' activities are provided by the pupils themselves in that they are responsible for developing their own design briefs in response to the stimulus and context. The risk management is provided by the interaction of the groups of pupils with the teacher.

There is no doubt that the products conceived by the pupils show creativity. They are original and of value. The pupils have clearly used their imaginations and have pursued their own purposes in developing the designs. Here the teacher has challenged the conventional approaches and organised the teaching so that the pupils work in groups (as opposed to individually), design (as opposed to design *and* make) and use new or emerging technologies as a starting point. The group work and resulting discussions enabled the pupils to take ownership of the work and develop design briefs that met their own personal interests. Their response was creative and rigorous in that the design proposals are for objects of worth, of benefit to those who will use them, acceptable to society and feasible both in terms of the way they will work and their desirability within the marketplace.

Summary and discussion

The act of designing has been shown to meet the criteria for creative activity as established by the report *All Our Futures: Creativity, Culture and Education* (Department for Education and Employment 1999). The findings of the QCA Nuffield Curriculum Centre seminar on the classroom conditions for creativity have been presented. A simple means of auditing the design decisions likely to be made by pupils in tackling a designing and making assignment (DMA) has been detailed.

In describing and discussing the design activity of pupils within design & technology at Key Stage 2 and Key Stage 3, I have tried to reveal the practice underlying their creativity in terms of the design decisions they make and the way the teacher has enabled the pupils to make them, and organised the teaching to meet the classroom conditions for creativity.

It is possible for pupils in Key Stage 2 and Key Stage 3 to act creatively when designing and making. The level of creativity will depend on the extent to which they are able to make design decisions, which can be made in any of the following areas: conceptual; technical; aesthetic; constructional; and marketing. It is unlikely that they will be able to make conceptual design decisions. It is important that the teacher controls the range of decisions that they make in the other four areas so that the teaching can provide the pupils with the intellectual and practical resources to make effective design decisions in these areas. The teacher can do this by orchestrating the teaching so that it meets the classroom conditions for creativity. The level of creativity achieved by the pupils can be gauged by looking at the diversity of response achieved within a class, simply by comparing the work of different pupils. If a class is producing work in response to a DMA that is uniform and lacking in flair then it is likely that the activity is over-structured, lacking in risk and with insufficient attention paid to context and stimulus. If a class is producing work in response to a DMA in which there is wide diversity but in which much, if not most, is unfinished, then the work is under-structured. It is the balance between restriction and choice made by the teacher and the way that this is managed to include some element of risk that will enable pupils to be creative in designing and making. The work of the Young Foresight Project has shown that if the need to make is removed, then the possibility of conceptual design decisions becomes a reality, with pupils in Year 9 responding positively and effectively when working in groups.

Without creativity the promise of design and technology will be reduced to the acquisition of technical skills without purpose. This is not the intention for the subject in the National Curriculum for England as this extract from the section on the importance of design and technology demonstrates:

> Pupils learn to think and intervene creatively to improve quality of life. The subject calls for pupils to become autonomous and creative problem-solvers, as individuals and members of teams.
>
> (Department for Education and Employment/Qualifications and Curriculum Authority 1999: 15)

Establishing creativity in the classroom is a priority for design and technology if it is to respond to this challenge.

Further reading

Barlex, D. *et al.* (2000) *Nuffield Design and Technology Teacher's File*. Harlow: Longman.

Buchanan, R. (1996) 'Wicked problems in design thinking', in V. Margolin and R. Buchanan (eds) *The Idea of Design*. Cambridge, MA: MIT Press, pp. 31–42.

Churchman, C.W. (1967) 'Wicked problems'. *Management Science*, 14(40), 141–2.

Cross, N. (2002) 'The nature and nurture of design ability', in G. Owen-Jackson (ed.) *Teaching Design and Technology in Secondary Schools: A Reader*. London: RoutledgeFarmer, pp. 124–39.

Cross, N., Naughton, J. and Walker, D. (1986) 'Design method and scientific method', in A. Cross and R. McCormick (eds) *Technology in Schools*. Milton Keynes: Open University, pp. 19–33.

Department for Education and Employment (1999) *All Our Futures: Creativity, Culture and Education.* London: DfEE/NACCCE.

Department for Education and Employment/Qualifications and Curriculum Authority (1999) *Design and Technology: The National Curriculum for England.* London: HMSO.

Ropohl, G. (1997) 'Knowledge types in technology'. *International Journal of Technology and Design* Education, 7(1, 2), 65–72.

For more on the Young Foresight Project featured in this chapter, see www.youngforesight.org.

CHAPTER

Creativity through geography

Fran Martin

'Create the future – don't just let it happen.'

(Birmingham DEC 1999)[1]

'Geographical education should build upon and shape the child's *own* experiences of the world.'

(Spencer and Blades 1993, my emphasis)[2]

THIS CHAPTER AIMS TO establish how and why geography has such great potential as a subject that can develop creative thinking in ways that are meaningful and relevant to children's own lives. It does so by examining the creative value of geography in three contexts – the subject, the teacher and the learner, illustrated with examples from classroom practice. Although the chapter focuses on creativity through geography, one example also draws on the historical enquiry process because aspects of historical enquiry can strengthen the type of geographical learning that relies on secondary sources.

Being creative about the subject

A common misconception about geography is that it is about being able to locate (or name) capital cities, major rivers, mountain ranges and other features on a globe or in an atlas. This rather narrow view of geography has pervaded society to such an extent that children's lack of locational knowledge is often reported in the press as a shocking indictment of the standard of geography teaching in schools.[3] In a piece of research into primary children's ideas about geography, one Year 6 pupil said: 'Geography is about islands, countries and landscape. You can learn a lot from geography about the UK and lots of other countries in the world. Sometimes you can learn about rivers, and it also helps you with your map reading. It is an important thing to learn about when you're going on holiday and you're the map reader.'[4]

While knowledge about countries, landscapes and skills such as map work are important, they are only one aspect of geography. Geography also has the potential to contribute to the development of a range of creative thinking skills, which in turn enable us to envision a variety of possible and preferred worlds. As Spencer and Blades (1993) point out, what often appears to be valued in geography (as indicated in the focus of assessment) is the uptake of information and gains in knowledge, whereas what is really of value is the *use* of that knowledge. As far back as 1975, Goodey was advocating that:

> Geography should be experiential, and should link up with issues such as the individual's experience of planning and environmental decision-making; their appreciation of the aesthetic and social qualities of townscapes and landscapes; and their involvement in discussion of social problems and the environment.[5]

Creative interpretations of the National Curriculum

As indicated above, for as many people that you ask 'What is geography?', you are likely to get as many different answers. Clearly people perceive geography in a variety of ways. Why does this matter when the curriculum (the National Curriculum in England) sets out what is supposed to be taught at each key stage? There can be no argument about the organising framework for geography in the curriculum, or can there? The framework for the National Curriculum Programmes of Study (DfEE/QCA 1999) is quite clear in its headings:

1   Geographical enquiry and skills

2   Knowledge and understanding of places

3   Knowledge and understanding of patterns and processes

4   Knowledge and understanding of environmental change and sustainable development

How, then, is it possible to be creative about a subject that is prescribed?

I would like to illustrate by giving two contrasting views of geography and its purpose as a subject in the curriculum.

1. Geography is about knowing where places are in the world and how the world 'works' in relation to the interaction between the human and physical environments

In this view, knowledge and understanding is emphasised and geographical skills are developed, such as those needed to conduct fieldwork and other investigations. Maps, as a means of communicating locational and spatial information, are a key resource. The overall aim of geography here is to develop a breadth and depth of knowledge and understanding about the world along with some important life skills. Knowledge is certain, unproblematic and not open to debate. In particular, 'knowledge is seen to have an objective reality without reference to a "knower"' (Posch and Rauch 1998: 256).[6] Here geography is seen as a subject in which children can learn about the world, and as one that is somehow separate from their own experiences. The role of the teacher might be conceptualised as an 'expert' who passes on his or her knowledge to the 'novice' child. The only problem is deciding which bits of the world to teach about, given the seemingly unlimited scope from local to global scales. Geography is easily assessable because teachers are clear about what the 'answers' are.

2. Geography is about seeing the world as a geographer who aims to create a better world

In this view, all people – adults and children alike – are geographers because they interact with the world on a daily basis and build up what Bale (1987)[7] has called their own 'private geographies' in which they have made – and continue to make – personal sense of the world around them. The purpose of geography is to help children make sense explicitly of, and build upon, these private geographies so that they might live as responsible global citizens able to act positively for a sustainable future. Personal meaning, in a social context, is central to this approach where children make connections between self and others, local with global. In this respect knowledge is constantly open to change and is 'conceived as a construct, actively made by each learner as he/she revises a conceptual map he/she uses to interpret the world' (Posch and Rauch 1998: 256). The role of the teacher is to draw on children's private geographies, using them as the starting point for geographical enquiries in which a conceptual framework is provided to help children make sense of the knowledge and skills they have acquired and to *create new understandings*. This is a collaborative venture in which the roles of teacher and learner become blurred and where there are many alternative 'answers', some of which are more appropriate than others.

These two quite contrasting views represent a continuum, and most people will have a view of geography that is somewhere along this line. However, I would like to propose that the closer your view is to the second, the more likely it is that you will be able to promote creativity through your teaching. Table 9.1 shows how the two views might interpret that part of the National Curriculum: Geography that focuses on *Place* – Programme of Study (PoS) 3.

In the first, the emphasis is on knowledge; in the second the emphasis is on personal knowledge and understanding, values and perspectives. The second is far more likely to promote creative thinking about places.

This is not to devalue the role of knowledge; it is important to be able to name, recognise and describe phenomena before you can create new meanings about them

TABLE 9.1 Two interpretations of PoS 3

Geography PoS 3: Knowledge and Understanding of Places

Interpretation 1: knowing where places are in the world – the sort of encyclopaedic knowledge of pub quizzes and *Mastermind* – and being able to describe them accurately.

Interpretation 2: identifying aspects of a place that give it its character, naming features of a place that the children value, bringing in the possibility of a variety of responses to the question 'What do we know about this place?'

and from them. However, it needs to be recognised that all knowledge is socially and culturally situated. For example, in the UK we use two words for what is described as cold, wet precipitation that falls as white flakes and settles of the ground: snow and slush. The Inuit – living in the arctic circle – have several different words enabling them to make distinctions between wet, slushy, soft and dry, hard compacted etc., because a finer-grained distinction in the language is necessary when you live in a cold country that is affected by snow all year round. In addition, if all geography lessons only focused on knowledge and skills, rather than moving on to the uncertain, debatable, value-laden elements, promotion of creativity and creative thinking skills would not be possible. Creativity requires us to:

- play with ideas;

- look at the known differently;

- question the accepted;

- create meanings and own them for ourselves; and

- be aware of, and open to, possibilities and perspectives.

In short, creativity in geography helps us to 'travel with a different view' (Slater 1992).[8]

What does a creative view of geography mean in practice?

'Geography, to me, is a subject which teaches us about the world, continents, countries and us. It helps us to learn about the Great Wall of China or the Eiffel Tower. It helps us to learn who we really are.'

(Year 6 pupil)[9]

In Chapter 1, Robert Fisher relates creativity to imagination: 'The world as it is presented to us is not the only possible world. Through our imagination we can use it as a model for other possible worlds.' A key *purpose* for creativity is also offered, showing that it is 'essential for citizens – living in changing and challenging social environments' and that creative skills are 'needed to manage conflicts of interest and argument, to understand others and resolve conflict'. I would add to this that we also live in changing and challenging *physical* environments and that these also lead to conflicts of interest that need resolving. Geography is a subject that brings the social (human) and physical together; it enables children to develop an understanding of the diverse ways people live in, are affected by and affect the world, and that this diversity, whilst being something to value and celebrate, can lead to inequalities, and therefore conflicts. From here it is possible, through imagining other possible worlds, to consider how conflicts and issues might be resolved, and the parts that individuals and groups might play in this process.

I believe this is what gives geography (and history) its purpose: to enable children to create new understandings or 'to travel with a different view' in order to make the world a better place.

Enabling children to travel with a different view in geography means:

- starting with children's own knowledge of, and interests in, the world;
- building on and extending their knowledge;
- problematising this knowledge, for example by identifying an issue, or by being critical of the sources of information (e.g. asking questions such as: 'Who produced this resource? For what purpose? What does it show? What does it not show?');[10]
- raising children's awareness of their own perspective on the issue;
- gaining understanding of a variety of perspectives on the same issue;
- using these perspectives (including their own) to generate a number of solutions / ideas about how to address the issue;
- making judgements about / evaluating alternative solutions; and
- making decisions about courses of action and justifying them.

These could be said to provide the learning objectives for children's creativity in geography.

What teaching and learning approaches can support these objectives?

During the late 1990s, David Leat[11] led a research project on a thinking skills approach to the teaching of geography. Originally, the research focused on geographical work at Key Stage 3, but later it expanded to look at other subjects and to apply and adapt the approaches for the primary school curriculum. The thinking skills approaches advocated are useful for creative thinking because the activities are *open-ended* and allow for *any number of responses*, as long as the children can *justify* them. Chapter 1 identified and discussed a number of processes involved in creative thinking, among which are possibility, rather than probability; *an* answer, rather than *the* answer; open-ended, rather than closed; and associative, rather than linear. 'Thinking through Geography' approaches make full use of these processes as well as drawing on critical thinking skills as and when appropriate. The approaches encourage the generation of alternatives, after which selections can be made according to whether they are more or less likely, more or less appropriate, or more or less helpful. The other strength of 'Thinking through Geography' approaches is in their emphasis on *debriefing* – that aspect of an activity which makes the process explicit and supports the children in learning how to learn – metacognition. Children are encouraged to evaluate their own performance and to identify not only what they feel they have learnt, but also what strategies they used that were helpful or not helpful. In this way a bank of strategies can be built that children can draw on in future situations.

In geography, much of this takes place through geographical enquiry which, at its simplest, has been defined as 'asking questions and finding answers using data sources' (Martin 1999).[12] These enquiries can focus on places, patterns and processes, and geographical issues. An enquiry in one area might well lead on to another. For example, an enquiry into land use – geographical patterns – might help children to identify an issue about why the land is used in this way and whether it meets the needs of the whole community, or not – a geographical issue.

Using key questions as a focus for critical and creative thinking

In 2002 I worked with a Year 2 teacher in a West Midlands primary school on adapting one of the Qualification and Curriculum Authority's units of work for geography (QCA 1998, 2000).[13] The teacher was interested in making the geography unit on a distant place beyond the United Kingdom more interesting and relevant to the children. In order to adapt the unit of work we put aside traditional approaches to planning and teaching a distant locality unit by thinking more creatively about the nature of geography and how it might best be taught. Table 9.2 shows the key questions we devised that provided the focus for learning at each stage in the unit, and the final column shows the types of activities and thinking required to help the children answer these questions.

Often, the types of key questions used in a unit of work about a distant place are those such as 'Where is this place?', 'What sort of place is it?', 'What is the weather like?', 'What do people do for work/leisure?', 'What is home/school life like?' and so on. The changes that we made to the unit can be summed up as a change in perspective. The key questions focus on the *process* of learning about a place that is beyond direct experience, rather than the *content* of that place. *What* the children learn remains the same – e.g. the physical and human features that are characteristic of St Lucia, such as the Pitons (volcanic mountains) and sulphur springs; how people in St Lucia live – what their homes are like and why; and what people in families do for work, leisure and education. *How* the children learn these things is different.

In order to achieve our revised aims we thought about whether there were historical skills that could be used to enhance a geographical enquiry. These were the skills of historical interpretation (PoS 3) and historical enquiry (PoS 4). The ability to move from identification and description to inference and deduction are central to historical interrogation of sources and we felt that these skills would enhance children's ability to make sense of distant places through the resources available to them.

Developing critical thinking using maps and photographs

When interpreting the maps, one child was able to identify that the maps showed St Lucia has an airport, many hotels and beaches for swimming, and then to deduce that people might go on holiday there. Another was able to identify that some hotels were close to the mountains and it might be very pretty there, so people would like to go

TABLE 9.2 Geography Unit – a contrasting localities overseas: Castries, St Lucia

Session	Key enquiry question	Types of thinking involved
1	How can we show what our locality is like to people from another area?	Building on knowledge already developed in earlier unit on 'Our local area', use creative thinking skills to make a photopack with maximum 20 photos, 2 maps and some writing.
2	What do we think St Lucia might look like?	Creative activity – imagining based on prior experience (to establish possible misconceptions held).
3	What do maps tell us about life in St Lucia?	Critical thinking skills used to interpret photos and develop a sound foundation of knowledge and understanding of life in a distant locality.
4	What do photos tell us about life in Castries, St Lucia? What do the photos not tell us? What would we like to know more about?	
5	What is life like in Castries, St Lucia? What does it mean to belong to this place?	
6	How is St Lucia similar / different to the place we live in? Why is this?	
7	How is St Lucia connected to where we live and the UK? (e.g. through food, holidays, relatives, story books etc.)	
8	What do we like / not like about the area we live in? What do the Harveys like / not like about the area they live in?	Critical thinking skills to make judgements about the quality of environments.
9	How might we choose to improve our area / quality of life?	Creative thinking skills used to imagine, generate (and be critical of) and model 'other possible worlds'. Activities focus on identifying key factors affecting the issue of quality of life and using this as basis for generating solutions.
10	How might people in Castries, St Lucia choose to improve their area / quality of life? (Perspectives of Harvey family, hi-tech communications factory worker, fisherman and tourist officer explored.) (This to extend to 2–3 lessons depending on time needed for ideas to develop.)	
11	Who will benefit from our ideas? Which solution will improve the quality of life of most people?	Critical thinking skills used to make judgements about ideas. Creative thinking skills used to develop favoured solution into a detailed model / report.

walking in the mountains. When interpreting the photographs the children identified that the people in them are smiling so they must be happy and like living in St Lucia. One photograph showed that the houses are made of corrugated iron so the children thought people in St Lucia might be poor, but they also noticed that the houses had telephone and electric wires so they must have electricity. This was confirmed in another photograph that showed a teenager in her living room with a TV. These are examples of critical thinking where the children were analysing the evidence and applying logic to come up with ideas about the place represented in the maps and photographs. At the same time the children were confirming some, and challenging other, preconceptions they had about what life might be like there.

Developing creative thinking using photographs

Two examples of activities using photographs that led to more creative responses are *Connections* and *Odd One Out*. For both of these games the children have sets of about ten photographs of St Lucia that are numbered. Each group of three or four children has the same set. The subject matter of the photos can vary according to what the purpose for learning is, and the photo sets can be made up of black-and-white reduced photocopies of the original set. Examples of photo sets that can be made from the St Lucia pack are: family life, buildings, the banana industry, life by the sea, landscapes and living in St Lucia.

1. *Connections*: Ask groups to place the photos together in pairs according to something that they think connects them or is similar. Each group then says what pairs they have made *and why*. Groups soon realise that many combinations of pairs are possible, and that some groups may have made a similar pair but identified a different connection. This is a creative activity because it is open-ended, and encourages the exploration of a number of possibilities and associations.

2. *Odd One Out*: Each group chooses three photos from the set of ten at random. They then decide which is the odd one out and why, thus identifying what is similar about two and different about the third. The range of possibilities after that might be to keep the same three photos and choose another odd one out, to add another photo to the set of three but keep the same odd one out, to select another three photos at random, and so on.

In these activities there is no 'right' answer. The children are, by doing this activity, creating their own set of 'criteria' or 'characteristics' of St Lucia. If the photos also contained those of the children's own UK locality, it would help them to distinguish between the two places, but also to identify in how many ways the places are similar. This helps create a much more fluid sense of place, and one which the children have created themselves rather than 'learnt' as a piece of knowledge. Another benefit of this approach is that it helps develop children's confidence in risk-taking. A child was heard to say, while working on one of these activities, 'Let's just try it and see', indicating a degree of confidence when tackling an activity in which there were elements of ambiguity.

Travelling with a different view: children's creative responses to a geographical issue

In the examples above, children are able to become explicitly aware of how they develop knowledge about places *on the basis of the evidence available to them*. In this way they are far more likely to realise that knowledge about places is both partial and subjective, because the sources themselves are partial and subjective, and because each person will have an element of subjectivity in the way they interpret a source. The children, therefore, become aware of their own perspectives and those of others around them, which, in turn, helps to add complexity to the subject matter being studied. The example below demonstrates how problematising knowledge can then enable children to be far more creative in their responses to a geographical issue, precisely because they are beginning to travel with a different view.

Working collaboratively to sort statements

A Year 3 class in Worcestershire were comparing their own place, a village, with Worcester, a city. They had already done fieldwork in both locations, drawn comparisons between the two using word maps, and drawn some initial conclusions about the nature and quality of life in each place. The teacher was then interested in helping the children to apply what they had learnt in a creative way by simulating a possible situation. A brief description of the activity is shown in Table 9.3.

The children had read through all of the statements in their literacy lesson that morning, so any complex words and ideas had already been discussed. They now worked in groups of three with an envelope of 16 statements and two cards saying YES and NO. The teacher modelled strategies for collaborative learning – 'You will need to share the statements. What I would like to hear is "Tyler, would you like to go first?" ' – and stressed that there was no right answer, and that each group could decide for themselves. 'Yes, the couple should move house, or no, they are better off staying in their flat in Worcester'. In the initial stages the children were sorting their statements quite quickly into their piles of 'yes' and 'no'.

They were clearly motivated and the groups' composition – mixed-ability to avoid literacy difficulties – and size enabled everyone to take part. After a while it became obvious that some groups were creating a third set of statements. As one group explained, 'we had to put it in the middle because some of it is yes and some of it is no', referring to statement 3 in Table 9.3 above. Another child drew on his own knowledge of the area and said about statement 4, 'The nearest hospital is in Bromsgrove because my gran went there, so we should put this statement on the side because it isn't right'. At this point the teacher got out a road atlas (see Figure 9.3) and the children were able to identify that Bromsgrove was much nearer to Hanbury than Worcester. Observations such as these were shared with the whole class during the midway debrief.

TABLE 9.3   Solving the problem – should Sultan and Shanta move house?

The brief	Sultan and Shanta are 27 years old. They are married and live in a small, two-bedroom flat above a video hire shop in Worcester. They would like to have children and are thinking about whether to move to a bigger house.
Sequence of activities	Task is explained. Children work in groups of three; each group has an envelope with a number of statements. Groups read through the statements and begin to sort them into piles of 'Yes, they should move' and 'No, they should not move'. Initial debrief after about 20 minutes. Groups continue to sort statements. Final debrief.
Examples of statements	**1.** Shanta walks to work in a bookshop near the centre of Worcester. Sultan drives to Birmingham every day, where he works at Aston Villa Football Club. They both work five days a week. **2.** Most of their friends live within walking distance. Most of their families live in Birmingham and they get together at least once a week. **3.** They have visited a house for sale in a village called Hanbury, 12 miles north of Worcester. It has three bedrooms, a garden and a garage. It would cost them more to live there because of a bigger mortgage. **4.** The nearest hospital to Hanbury is in Worcester. **5.** The house in Hanbury looks out onto fields and is one mile from the village centre. The air is very fresh.
Midway debrief questions	What are you doing / how are you doing the task? Are some statements more helpful than others? Examples? Reasons? Have any of you moved from the city to the country? Do you know why you moved? What ideas have we gained that can help us carry on with the task?
Final debrief questions	Should Sultan and Shanta move to the village or not? What statements helped you make this decision? Did everyone in your group agree? If not, how did you come to a final decision? Was there some information that you would have liked that the statements didn't give you? Do some statements seem to be more important than others? Why?

Children sharing their own perspectives and being critical of the sources of information

In the final debrief, groups were split between whether they thought the couple should move or not. Those who thought they should move reasoned that 'there is too much pollution in the town; they need a bigger house for the children', while those who

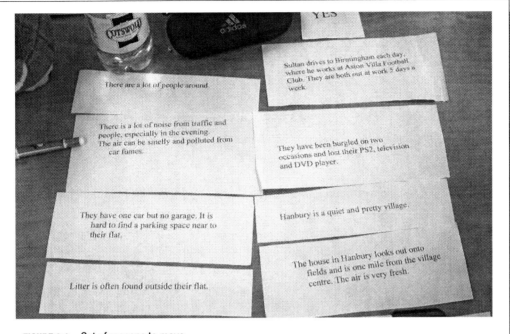

FIGURE 9.1 Set of reasons to move

FIGURE 9.2 Creating a third set

thought they should not move did so because 'there are more shops and things to do in Worcester; there are more parks for children in Worcester'. John had clearly worked out his ideas: 'I've got three reasons why they should move: 1. because they get burgled in

FIGURE 9.3 Checking information in an atlas

Worcester; 2. because the air is bad; 3. because there is a bigger house in Hanbury for children'. Some children were undecided because they could see both sides of the argument. These children, particularly, had become much more aware of how complex the issue was and that there was no simple, 'correct', answer. Most of the children were also able to identify information that they would have found useful but that was not provided on the statements: 'House prices should have been given'; 'Are there bigger houses in Worcester?'; 'How many children is Shanta going to have?'; and 'We don't know if there are any secondary schools in Hanbury'.

Considering perspectives and generating solutions

The children were also able to draw the conclusion that if Sultan and Shanta decided not to move to Hanbury that did not mean they should not move at all. For example, one child suggested that the couple might move to a bigger house that was still in Worcester but further away from the city centre. On this basis the teacher planned to do a role play that would enable the children to become aware of other people's perspectives on the issue and to identify some possible solutions. The roles identified were:

- The Estate Agent, who would have a map of the area and a variety of house details collected from estate agents in and around Worcester. The estate agent would have to think about what advice would be given to Sultan and Shanta about where they could look next.

- Sultan and Shanta, who would also have some house details and be asked to think about what they would say to their estate agent.

- Sultan and Shanta's family and friends who would have brief information cards about themselves and their relationship to the couple. They would have to think about where they might like the couple to move to and why.

Once they have considered the various perspectives the children will be able to devise a range of alternative solutions to the original question and then evaluate each before deciding which alternative might be the most appropriate and why.

Time to think

The above example illustrates how creativity in geography can be fostered through devising activities that are motivating, inspirational and in which children work collaboratively. The fourth element needed to foster creativity, as identified in Chapter 1, is *gestation*. The sequence of activities in the example of Sultan and Shanta show how the teacher built in thinking time for the children, with the result that they were able to develop both breadth and depth of understanding of the issue. This was achieved through:

- creative use of teaching time – e.g. using the statements as the focus for the Literacy Hour;

- providing a clear focus for thinking – e.g. use of a key question to answer, and a clear brief for the role play;

- devising activities that required the children to do the thinking, rather than the teacher;

- the teacher scaffolding children's learning – e.g. through the use of targeted questioning that encouraged different types of thinking in the children[14]; and

- a clear sequence of activities spread over several days – literacy lesson to role play – giving prolonged thinking time, or gestation, between lessons.

The importance of creativity in geography

As pupils study geography, they encounter different societies and cultures. This helps them to realise how nations rely on each other. It can inspire them to think about their own place in the world, their values, and their rights and responsibilities to other people and the environment.

(DfEE/QCA 1999)[15]

Teaching over the last five years or so has not given much space for any foundation subject, let alone thinking time for children. The prescription and volume of the

National Curriculum and Primary Strategies have led to foundation subjects such as geography and history fighting for space and so making it appear as though there is even less time to 'cover' what is prescribed in the programmes of study. Teachers are faced with hard decisions about whether to go for breadth or depth in their selection of content. In addition, there is the pervading view that geography is a subject that focuses on the accumulation of knowledge about people, places and environments.

This chapter has attempted to put forward an alternative view of the subject which is child-centred and has a focus on values and attitudes as much as knowledge and skills, but is, none the less, rigorous in its approach to both the process of learning and its outcomes. Geography's importance beyond knowledge is evident in the quote above, and creativity is absolutely central to this approach. While the curriculum as a whole might place constraints on what is taught, there is also the view that the greater the constraints are, the more creative you need to become. The purpose of geography as a whole is clear. The examples in this chapter illustrate how promoting creativity through geography is not about asking children to 'imagine what it might be like to live in another place' but is about providing a clear framework, with selected resources, that engages children in a series of critical and creative processes. There is evidence of the creative processes of generation, variation and originality – although the originality may be individual or social rather than universal. There is also evidence of children demonstrating flexibility of thought, curiosity, and the ability to compare and to connect ideas and to question accepted ways of doing things.

All these aspects of creativity can be developed through geography. They are vital to the subject – in providing a sense of purpose and relevance to children's lives – and to the world at large. They are vital because they lead to a balanced approach to understanding how we live in the world that has the potential to create better understanding of social and environmental conflict, and therefore to lead to the creation of more appropriate solutions in the struggle to achieve a better world.

Acknowledgements

I would like to thank Bronwen Williams and the children of Year 2, Pitmaston School, Worcester, and Caroline Mathews and the children of Year 3, Welland Primary School, Worcestershire.

Notes

1 GeoVisions slogan for the debate on the future of school geography, Birmingham DEC (1999) *GeoVisions: Debate and Development – progress report on the first phase of GeoVisions 1998–99.*

2 Spencer, C. and Blades, M. (1993) 'Children's understanding of places: the world at hand', in *Geography*, **78**, 367–73.

3 For an example of how geography is reported in the press, see Rawling, E. (2001) *Changing the Subject*. Geographical Association.

4   Catling, S. and Brown, M. (1999) 'English primary schoolchildren's definitions of geography'. Unpublished paper presented at the Primary Geography Research Conference, Charney Manor, Oxfordshire, March 1999.

5   This quote from Goodey came from Spencer and Blades (1993: 367). Goodey's work on children's perceptions of the environment set a model that attempted to explain how children build up their knowledge and understanding of the world through a variety of direct and indirect experiences, between which there are constant interactions.

6   Posch, P. and Rauch, F. (1998) 'Developments in teacher education through environmental education research'. *International Research in Geographical and Environmental Education*, 7(3), 255–9.

7   Bale (1987) *Geography in the Primary School*. London: Routledge and Kegan Paul. Bale coined the phrase 'private geographies' as a means of conceptualising the geographical knowledge children build up internally as a result of their daily experiences of the world. These experiences could be direct/ first-hand or indirect/second-hand. Both types of experiences are equally valid as ones that teachers can build upon.

8   Slater, F. (1992) 'To travel with a different view', in Naish, M. (ed.) *Geography and Education*. Institute of Education, University of London, pp. 97–113.

9   Catling, S. (2001) 'English primary schoolchildren's definitions of geography', in *International Research in Geographical and Environmental Education*, 10(4), 363–78.

10 This is an example of geography drawing on historical skills to enhance learning. Learning about distant people and places relies on the use of secondary sources, each of which have also been 'filtered' by the people who wrote them, selected the photographs, decided what information to put on a map and what to leave out and so on. The skills of historical interpretation enable children to interrogate and be critical of such information sources.

11 Leat has edited a number of books in the 'Thinking Through . . .' series published by Chris Kington Publishing, www.chriskingtonpublishing.co.uk.

12 For a fuller analysis of geographical enquiry refer to Martin (1999) 'The enquiry approach: What why and how?' *Primary Geographer*, **38**, 4–8.

13 This was part of some work, commissioned by the QCA in 2002, on adapting two units from QCA (1998, 2000) *Scheme of Work for Key Stages 1 & 2: Geography*. London: QCA.

14 'Scaffolding' is the term used by Bruner (cited in Leat 1998) to describe the process of enabling a child to progress to a higher level of achievement. The use of frameworks for different types of thinking can be found in Martin (1998) and Martin and Mathews (2002).

15 Quote from 'The Importance of Geography' statement in DfEE/QCA (1999) *The National Curriculum for England: Geography*. London: DfEE/QCA.

Further reading

Catling, S. (2003) 'Curriculum contested: primary geography and social justice', in *Geography*, 88, 164–210.

Higgins, S. and Baumfield, V. (2001) *Thinking Through the Primary Curriculum*. Cambridge: Chris Kington Publishing.

Leat, D. (1998) *Thinking Through Geography*. Cambridge: Chris Kington Publishing.

Martin, F. (1999) 'The enquiry approach: What Why and How?' *Primary Geographer*, 38, 4–8.

Martin, F. (2002a) 'Primary historians and geographers learning from each other'. *Primary History*, 32, 18–21.

Martin, F. (2002b) 'Thinking skills and developing understanding about place', in Bowles, R. (ed.) *Raising Achievement in Primary Geography: Occasional Paper 2*. London: Register of Research in Primary Geography, pp. 57–62.

Martin, F. and Mathews, C. (2002) 'Thinking through the QCA Units of Work', in *Primary* Geographer, 47, 12–14.

Martin, F. and Owens, P. (2004) 'Geography in the foundation stage', in Scoffham, S. (ed.) *Handbook of Primary Geography (2nd edn)*. Geographical Association.

10

Creativity in music and art

Sara Liptai

'How should we promote creativity in the arts?'

IN TERMS OF CONVENTIONAL thinking about creativity this chapter might seem superfluous since arts subjects, by definition, give children the scope to express themselves with freedom, originality, often without words and, much of the time, without reference to pencil and paper. However, given a rich concept of creativity (as delineated in Chapter 1), this chapter argues that the teaching of music and art lend themselves to exploration and collaborative work in ways that may have been neglected or simply not thought to be part of the teaching/learning agenda. It seeks to shows how children can be empowered to participate more actively in their education, through dialogue and setting some of their own learning agenda.

The arts curriculum, traditionally (and in the National Curriculum), focuses on 'making' and 'doing' rather than 'talking about'. Having finally managed to get away from the dominance of words in arts subjects, why should anyone want to go back to a word-bound pattern of arts education? This chapter explores the benefits of philosophical enquiry into children's education in the arts. The approach being advocated here is the introduction of a special kind of regular group or class *discussion* during music and art lessons in a format called the 'community of enquiry'. The 'collaborative conversation' that takes place in a community of enquiry is shown to be a source of effective, creative and sustained learning for children and young people.

Activating latent knowledge and understanding

Today's children seem to possess high levels of unconscious, unacknowledged visual and aural literacy. This is the natural consequence of the great deal of television, video and/or computer game consumption experienced by virtually all children in this country. Most teachers will be aware of children's high ability to read visual clues, including subtle ones, for example in cartoons. What may be less obvious to teachers – except to those with special interest in this area – is children's equally high ability in perceiving and interpreting aural or musical clues.

For example, in Raymond Briggs's feature-length cartoon, *The Snowman*, apart from the famous song at the end there are no words, only continuous orchestral accompaniment (composed by Howard Blake). In it there is a scene in which the little boy and the Snowman, who had magically come to life, creep upstairs in the middle on the night to nose around the parents' bedroom. The Snowman finds the dad's dentures and tries them out. Here the music becomes rather strange. I asked two groups of primary-age children, a Year 3 and a Year 4 class, to interpret the scene. Both groups explained, without hesitation, that the music expressed the Snowman's mixed feelings, including fascination and revulsion, on glimpsing himself in the mirror with the dentures.

To reach such a subtle, yet unequivocal, interpretation, the children needed to have fluent understanding of the compositional conventions and meanings of western classical music, and needed to know how to relate visual and musical clues to one another. How can this kind of, largely hidden, knowledge be captured, activated and built into music education? Philosophical enquiry can help children to do this and also help them to deal judiciously with the barrage of messages from audio-visual media that bombard them daily.

Addressing the big questions about the arts

Not only are commercial pressures put on them, but today's children are also surrounded by a multiplicity of definitions, interpretations and conventions about the arts. What is high art to one set of people seems like incoherent scribblings ('a monkey could have done it') to another. What is experienced as soothing and fulfilling music by one person might be heard as sentimental rubbish by someone else. The height of modern fashion may appear to some as a grotesque distortion of the concept of making and wearing clothes. While some find contemporary arts and crafts aesthetically pleasing, others prefer antiques. Any work of art can present us with challenging questions.

How are children supposed to make sense of the world of the arts? How can they find out what is art and what is not? How will they understand why the judges of the Turner Prize honour conceptual art? How can they interpret the different cultural conventions that put steel pans, brass bands, string quartets and rock groups side-by-side at school concerts? Where will they get criteria for what makes one design 'cool', another one 'twee'? How can they interrogate the concept of taste? How can they tell the kitsch peddled by the heritage industry from old objects of real worth? Such philosophical/ aesthetic and sociological questions about the arts are not only of great interest to children; they also constitute essential learning for them.

At present there is no provision for the systematic interrogation of such questions in the arts curriculum. Therefore, by default, such questions tend to arise, if at all, only in the home. The introduction of philosophical/aesthetic enquiry, based on children finding or identifying such questions, offers all children opportunities to ponder about, clarify and share their ideas and, as a consequence, grow in understanding of creativity in the arts while also developing their thinking skills.

Supporting the individual child in developing his/her artistic tastes

When children are given a forum and a challenge for discussing and making sense of their experiences and understandings in the arts, they often value the experience. It also seems to enhance the thoughtfulness and depth of their own artwork that follows a rigorous, yet open-minded, interrogation of works of art and artistic experiences. For example, in a recently published teaching resource: *Ta(l)king Pictures: Thinking Through Photography*, the quality of the children's art work in Year 3 and 5 is so high that, without the captions, it is not always easy to tell which photographs were taken by children and which ones are by adult photographic artists.[1]

Discussing their interpretations of media messages in the arts gradually leads children to greater understanding of the messages and their own responses to them. Group discussion offers them a creative forum for exploring themselves in relation to various aspects of the arts, including their own artistic activities, their tastes and also the artistic conventions, habits and preferences arising from their individual ethnic and cultural backgrounds. The understanding thus acquired will inform their subsequent artistic activities both in and out of school, as well as their understanding of themselves as unique individuals within a cultural, ethnic, sociological context. They will be using their creativity to construct a richer, better informed, more sophisticated understanding of who they are. Philosophical enquiry about the arts, or aesthetic enquiry, provides an ideal forum for such a creative endeavour.

The Community of Enquiry

Philosophical enquiry, or *Philosophy for Children*, is an approach to developing children's thinking. It takes place in the intellectually rigorous, but emotionally and socially supportive, environment. The environment is a format or structure for group discussion, which Lipman called 'the community of enquiry'.[2]

The discussion proceeds through the joint exploration of the philosophical or aesthetic question chosen by the participants. They take turns offering their ideas and opinions, supported by reasoning, to the rest of the group. The participants listen to, and agree or disagree with, build on, expand, add a different dimension to, or criticise each other's ideas. The discussion moves forward indirectly, like a boat tacking into the wind, and this forward movement is what, in Lipman's view, distinguishes an aesthetic enquiry from a mere conversation. It has its own rules and procedures.

Setting and rules

The usual setting of the community of enquiry is a circle or horse-shoe shape, to enable all participants to have eye contact with each other. The teacher/facilitator sits as part of the circle. Rules are agreed and recorded. These are similar to general classroom behaviour rules, but their focus is on helping to establish both procedures and emotional safety within the group, e.g. 'only one person speaks at a time' and 'no nasty put-downs'.

The stimulus

The facilitator introduces the stimulus. The choice of the stimulus is the point at which the facilitator has influence over the content of the enquiry (in Lipman's programme this is a section of a philosophical novel).

Thinking time

The participants are asked to contemplate the stimulus, usually in silence, in order to identify features they find interesting or puzzling, perhaps disturbing.

Formulating questions

Participants are invited to put their ideas about the stimulus into the form of questions, which are recorded verbatim. Questions can be formulated individually or in pairs. They can be compared and connections of meaning between them can be sought.

Choosing a question for discussion

This is most often done by a simple majority vote.

Discussion

Members of the community take turns sharing their ideas, relevant experience, arguments or examples in an effort to construct an answer to the chosen question. The participants build on each other's ideas, by adding to them or criticising them.

Conclusions, review

The cognitive outcome of the enquiry is, ideally, one of two kinds: a consensus about the best possible answer to the question that could be constructed under the circumstances, or a clarification of differences of opinion. However, most enquiries end up generating further questions, which can be explored on future occasions or in follow-up activities.

The role of the facilitator

The facilitator of a community of enquiry fulfils a different role from the teacher of a conventional lesson. While a teacher tends to be a source of information, the ultimate authority on subject knowledge and the judge of the quality of the knowledge of the child participants, the facilitator is a co-enquirer. His/her most important role is to encourage the discussion to move from the particular to the general, from the concrete to the abstract, i.e. always from lower- towards higher-order thinking skills and towards metacognitive understanding, while ensuring fair and equal participation for all.

The philosophical community of enquiry

It follows from the ethos of the community of enquiry that the questions under discussion have no single right answer. They are worthy of debate precisely because an answer to them has to be made up by drawing on the participants' experience, knowledge, beliefs and opinions. Any answer arrived at has to be seen as temporary, as the best that a particular community can construct at a particular moment, just like the answers given by professional philosophers to the 'big questions', for example, 'What is honesty?' 'What is beauty?' 'How do we know what we know?' As everyone has ideas, and has the right to express those ideas about such philosophical questions, a community of enquiry is a truly democratic place of learning where children can pose, and collaborate in finding answers for questions of their own choosing.

Aesthetic enquiry as a version of philosophical enquiry

The starting point or stimulus of an aesthetic enquiry is not a piece of philosophical text but a work of art: a piece or pieces, or excerpts, of music, painting, photographs, sculpture, craftwork, a design, an edifice, a dance or a mime. Aesthetic enquiry can also admit and investigate objects or genres that do not necessarily fall into the conventional aesthetic categories, e.g. advertisements, product catalogues, 'found objects', fragments, children's work, etc.

A work of art also has multiple meanings, including the artist's embodied meaning(s). Because of its non-verbal nature, discussions about works of art or craft are, of necessity, acts of translation. The deciphering of their meaning depends not only on the ability to think philosophically and to express these thoughts coherently, but also on the understanding of the cultural conventions that the works of art or craft refer to, as well as the understanding of the cultural context in which they had been created (see the example of children interpreting *The Snowman*'s music above).

A work of art as stimulus cannot simply be used as a springboard for discussion and then jettisoned; it requires repeated revisiting in order for new and deeper layers of meaning to be discovered. This repeated interrogation results in thorough acquaintance with the work of art – probably a rare experience for most children (except, perhaps, for active musicians). For children of different abilities and interests to have various works of art firmly lodged in their minds is an enriching experience, akin to knowing lots of poems or songs by heart. These thoroughly 'learned' works of art can become part of children's thinking repertoire as reference points and resources. They can start influencing aesthetic choices.

In enquiring into a work of art children are encouraged to consider their own aesthetic preferences, and other children's, and are encouraged to express what they think in relation to their own cultural context, and also to interrogate their own and others' contexts for deeper understanding.

Aesthetic enquiry is different from conventional discussions about the arts

Discussion about music or musical experience in conventional music lessons tends to be restricted to either impressionistic, metaphorical stuff of no great depth ('the music reminds me of a walk in the snowy forest') or thoroughly technical analysis according to the 'elements of music' listed in the National Curriculum Music document, e.g. structure, dynamics, texture (i.e. the number and kind of the different parts), timbre (the colour of the sound of the different parts or instruments used). This list is based on criteria created for theoretical purposes and not for helping youngsters make sense of their musical experience.

Aesthetic enquiry has the potential to bridge the gap between these two modes of engagement: the purely metaphorical and the purely technical, by encouraging children to create a language for describing and interrogating musical experience. This language is usually largely impressionistic at the beginning but, with the development of the community of enquiry, it admits more and more musical concepts. Children construct these concepts in order to describe musical experience ever more precisely. Once they have grasped the musical concepts, they seem to have no difficulty adopting the technical terms that label them. The exchanges between children in a mature community of enquiry are not dissimilar to the deliberations of a music or art critic who knowledgeably combines the impressionistic and metaphorical with technical description.

In summary, aesthetic enquiry encompasses much more than the usual appraising activities in music and art lessons. It opens up the philosophical dimensions of artistic experience, by:

- scrutinising the assumptions underlying the assessment of any object as a work of art;

- exploring the foundations of aesthetic understanding, cultural conventions, habits, learning, taste; and

- investigating not only the product, the work of art, but also the processes of artistic creation.

The enquiry approach to the teaching of music, art and design shows some similarities with the renowned Reggio Emilia arts project that toured Britain in the late 1990s. However, aesthetic enquiry goes a step further than the Italian project. It gives children the tools, in the form of critical and creative thinking – for articulating and interrogating their experiences of the arts, including their own pictures, artefacts and compositions. The constant interplay between looking or listening, creating and talking reinforces the connections between children's creative and logical, non-verbal and verbal, 'right-brain' and 'left-brain' capacities, and also catering for different learning styles.

Starting points for work with children

Images: likes and dislikes

1   Offer children a wide range of visual images: photographs, reproductions of paintings, greeting cards (sentimental, humorous, etc.), picture calendars, children's drawings or paintings, and perhaps also other materials: pieces of fabric, embroidery, lace, etc.

2   Ask children to choose one they like and one they dislike. If more than one child chooses an object they can start discussing their opinions about it with their fellow chooser(s).

3   Go round the circle and ask each child to explain his/her choices. Let other children add to, or comment, on the choices (constructively). Children are entitled to any opinion but they have to be able to offer a reason for it.

4   When the circle is completed, ask children what they have found out about others through their choices.

If it is a group that has been together for some time, ask what new and surprising knowledge has emerged. If it is a new class – and this is a particularly good introduction game – ask what children remember of other children's words, and why. Can they find a connection with their own experience? Why do they think they found a particular detail memorable? What is it about their own interests that is revealed by what they remember of others' interests? This game can develop into a full-scale aesthetic enquiry if desired.

This game is helpful for quiet and shy children because they can give of themselves indirectly, through their explanations about their choices. Surprising connections between children may emerge. The beginnings of a shared aesthetic language can be established. If more or less the same set of images can be assembled at the beginning and end of a reasonably long period of aesthetic enquiries, for example a school year, it can be used as a tool for teachers' assessment, as well as children's self-assessment, of the development of their visual interests, taste and vocabulary.

Games and enquiries with Christmas cards

With Foundation and Key Stage 1 children

Make a pile of Christmas cards. Ask the class to think about how the cards could be sorted or put into groups. Accept any grouping they suggest and sort the cards accordingly. It might help to stick to one way of grouping into two piles first, then to find a new category and re-sort. Keep a list of categories on the board. Decide whether or not to aim for binary categories (i.e. the presence or absence of an element e.g. gold).

Look at the list and sort in a range of categories, e.g. colour, subject matter (the objects depicted), religious/non-religious, art technique, mood (humorous/serious). Have a discussion or a proper enquiry (starting with a list of questions) about one of the categories or, rather, the cards in that category.

For children in Key Stages 2 and 3

Give each group a batch of Christmas cards to put into categories in as many different ways as they can. There will be cards that go into several categories. Ask each group to list its categories. Compare lists.

Ask the children to list the objects (symbols) on their cards, with their meaning(s), e.g. polar bears/penguins/robin; winter/cold/snow; the physical attributes of the season – pudding; folk/eating custom; cartoon of Three Wise Men; a non-religious/profane take on an element of the story; gold decoration; the first of the three presents, also riches, holiness – think of the background of Byzantine icons.

Discuss which of the symbols has meaning outside the context of Christmas and in other religions. What are these meanings, are they derived from the Christmas meaning, or independent of them (e.g. dove, the symbol of the Holy Spirit as well as of peace)? Which symbols have most significance for the children and why? Find parallels with symbols from other belief systems. Discuss the concept and use of symbols.

For higher-ability children

Ask the children to put a set of cards in order from the most seriously religious to the most profane. How can the subtle differences be expressed in words? Ask children to categorise the cards according to the style and age of the art work. Conduct an aesthetic enquiry about a small selection of cards representing different techniques/approaches/standards of taste.

Discuss how people choose Christmas cards, what their choice of cards says about them and what reasons there might be for sending cards. Go beyond the obvious ones.

An example of how this worked with a Year 2 class

A Year 2 class was asked to compare two Christmas cards. Both had a Christmas tree as their main image, but they were in different styles. The children were asked to identify similarities and differences by using the phrase 'They are similar because . . .' or 'They are different because . . .'. Then a few children were asked to choose three from many cards spread on the floor in front of them, and explain a connection between them. Without further scrutiny of the cards they were asked to list images that might be found on them. This is their list:

robins	snowflakes	Snow White	fairies
snowmen	Rudolf	snowballs	toys
Santa	stockings	holly leaves	Christmas
trees	(Santa) hats	tree balls (i.e.	songs
presents	Christmas	baubles)	crackers
snow	lights	sleigh	cake
stars	children	angels	tinsel
reindeer	candles	Jesus	

The facilitator queried 'Snow White'. The children, after considerable struggle, articulated the connection between the name of the fairy tale heroine and the Christmas weather conditions. The children were asked to look at the cards again and match the images to the list. The images identified on cards were ticked on the list and others added:

| crowns | God | kings |
| frog | penguins | bells |

Questioning by the facilitator revealed that most of the class was hazy about the connection between the crowns and the Christmas story, even though they will have participated in the school's Christmas play for several years, and the school's intake is almost exclusively English speaking and white. Once a higher-ability child had explained the connection, several sets of Three Kings were found on cards.

The frog spotted on another card was seated on a water-lily leaf, with mouth open and book in hand. With reference to 'Christmas songs' on the first list, the frog was identified as a carol singer. The penguins were explained as creatures permanently living under Christmas weather conditions.

The teacher pointed out that all the elements of both lists referred to the *pictures* on the cards, and asked how else the cards might be sorted. Looking at the plain back of two different cards prompted children to suggest *shape* as a category, within which they identified *squares* and *rectangles* and, within rectangles, *short* and *long*, meaning brick-shape and narrow ones. Two different square cards prompted the category of *size*. Then someone spontaneously offered the category of cards *with and without writing on (the front)*. Finally a child suggested *colour*.

In the follow-up session their list of Christmas images could have been organised into categories, i.e. *things to do with the Christmas story, customs, weather*. The creation and interrogation of categories is an essential part of encouraging higher- order think-ing in children. The rich and complex, but familiar, imagery of Christmas cards is a good vehicle for this. It also allows a great deal of personal experience to be sifted, sorted, shared and interrogated. It provides learning for children with non-Christian traditions. The game can, of course, be conducted with Eid, Rosh Hashana or Diwali greeting cards. Comparisons can be drawn between the religious stories and customs.

Creativity with found objects

Pass small objects – singly or in pairs or threes, identical or different – round the circle of children and ask how they might use the objects. Accept and celebrate both literal and fantastic solutions. For example, a Year 3 and 4 (vertically grouped) class of children were given three coloured plastic frustums (cones with their tips chopped off). These objects, light and about 20 cm in diameter, are generally used as markers during games. The opening, where the cone tip was missing, was just large enough for a child's fist to fit through. The children were asked to think of ways they could either *wear* or *use* these objects. The frustums were handed around the circle. Children explained and demonstrated their ideas, which included knee or elbow pads/protector, spectacles frame, Frisbee, a basket to be carried on one's head, decoration over/around a bobble, shoulder pads, a mask, a gas mask, an artist's hat, alien's face or mask, a loudspeaker, a set of drums, containers for sorting small objects, traffic-light covers, Chinese hat with air vent in the middle for protection in very hot weather, ankle protectors, bracelet, ankle bangles for dancing, breathing mask, a bib for a baby and musical instruments (for banging together).

This ten-minute playful activity shows the beginnings of the kind of artistic creativity for which the process of aesthetic enquiry is designed to foster. The connections with the teaching of design are obvious, but the aesthetic implications merit separate consideration. The reconceptualisation of the use of simple everyday objects and the ability to see these objects in new ways is fundamentally the same ability that artists have for reconceptualising and/or reinterpreting their environment. The emphasis in this activity was on fluidity, flexibility, lateral thinking, figurative thinking, symbolic thinking and all elements of creative thinking.

Collaborative masterpiece

Draw a line (straight or squiggle, zigzag, circle) on a large sheet of blank paper. Children take turns to add a line to the drawing. Either let children draw in silence or ask them to say how they are changing the picture as they are drawing their line. The drawing is finished when the child whose turn it is to draw declares it finished and gives it a title.

Variation: stop the drawing after every dozen lines and ask for a possible title. Questions for discussion include:

- What is a line? (difference between mathematical and artistic definition)

- What is the difference between finished and unfinished pictures?

- How has the picture changed between the temporary titles and the final one?

- What makes a picture?

- What makes an abstract picture?[3]

The discussions about what makes a picture and how we perceive images (how we know what title to give them) touch on profoundly philosophical topics, yet are accessible to all children.

Composing to a given 'graphic' score

Choose a range of images, for example art photos or reproductions of paintings of, e.g., landscapes, mosaic tiles, a humorous scene or an abstract painting. These images will constitute the 'graphic scores' of compositions. Each child should have the freedom to choose an image that speaks to them. The children who have chosen the same image can start discussing the composition in a group.

Pose the question 'How can the chosen image be depicted in music?' First of all, concentrate on the compositional idea. How do the children perceive the picture? Do they see it as one integrated image with one strong central impact, or as constructed of its parts? If it is one strong image, what is it about? What kind of emotional impact does it make? What kind of music might represent that impact best? Encourage the children to think of analogies. If there is one strong impact to make, how can that be broken into constituents of instrumental or vocal sounds? How can the simultaneity of parts of the image be translated into a composition that unfolds in time? What style? How long? How intense? What resources do they need? If the image is seen as a sum of its constituents, the compositional process is more transparent. How can the parts of the image be grasped: described, explained, one-by-one and in relation to each other? Which parts are bigger or more/less vivid or more/less important?

Once the image has been 'mapped', each part can be found a musical equivalent: a particular timbre, a phrase, a mode of expression, an instrument or a group of instruments. Next the 'route' of the composition needs to be decided. How are the constituents to be displayed? What is their best sequence? Are related or similar parts to be played next to each other or are they to be far apart? How will their similarities be made obvious? How can dynamics be used to help the process of displaying the parts? Is there to be a quiet start of relatively unimportant parts? Is there a crescendo? Can the sequence of parts be played in a different way? In the overall composition, should the sequence be played in more than one way?

When it comes to performance, it would be helpful to have the stimulus image available for the listeners to look at while listening to the composition. Can they see the connections between the image and the music? What do they like? What would they have done in a different way?

An example from a Year 5 class

In a Year 5 class two groups chose the same bare, ragged, mountainous winter landscape with a lake in the foreground. One of them composed some sort of a narrative sequence by allocating a different type of music to each section of the picture, and presenting these one after the other, with one child indicating which part of the photograph was 'being played'. The other group started with a similar, but shorter, sequence, following it with the musical depiction of the overall image, involving many different simultaneous sounds. A third group chose a circular pattern from a Roman mosaic floor, creating a composition in rondo form (ABACADA structure), where A indicated the recurring nature of the pattern.

The special feature of this way of teaching music is the constant focus on developing metacognitive self-awareness: the regular return to the abstract discussion; the wish to see things in context, in relation to each other and to the self; the constant negotiation between children, between solutions, approaches, impacts. If more than one group of children picks an image, and two compositions are prepared with the same 'score', a comparison of the two approaches could stimulate more creative thought and discussion.

Two pictures and two pieces of music

Choose two pictures and two pieces, or excerpts, of music. Children are asked to describe the two pictures, one-by-one as well as in comparison with each other. Play the first piece of music and ask the children which picture it might be connected with and why. Then play the second piece and ask the same question. Have any of the children changed their minds about the connections after hearing the second piece of music? When several children have made the same connection, do they give different reasons for it? Do they build on each other's ideas?

An example from a Year 2 class

The two pictures were 'Lily pond' by Claude Monet (P1) – the well-known painting of his garden with the green wooden bridge over the pond spanning the background – and 'Starry night' by Vincent van Gogh (P2), a landscape with a small, far-away village, dom-inated by swirling patterns in the sky and a single, nervous cypress in the foreground. Of the two pieces of music one was anxious film music by Phil Davies (M1), the other 'Une barque sur l'ocean', a varied, predominantly calm seascape by Maurice Ravel (M2).

This Year 2 class applied a range of techniques when making connections. Some children identified specific musical features and matched these with visual ones, for example:

'Ooh, ooh' in the pipes: smoke in the middle of the picture (Colin) [M1; P2]
'Ooh' not smoke but wind blowing in the night (Carl) [M1; P2]
Hitting a rock with a hammer (metaphor for drums?), getting louder (Josh) [M1; P2]
The music sounds like wind and there is wind in the picture (Sheila) [M1; P2]

Others reversed the process by picking out a feature or features of the picture(s) that matched the music:

> You can hear the stars and the wind blowing (Kay) [M1; P2]
> The village is haunted ... the bushes swing in the wind and the crickets are noisy (Nathan) [M1; P2]
> The music is like that bit of the picture (pointing at the water and grass) (Rob) [M1; P1];
> Sounds like the grass waving backwards and forwards (Josh)[M2; P1]
> [Sounds like] the wind is going round the stars and the moon (Jamie) [M1; P2]

Many children built a fantasy around the picture that matched the mood suggested by the music, adding elements to the picture that *might be* there in the context of the music. In other words, these children recontextualised the picture in response to music, for example:

> Someone on the trees is playing a blowing instrument (Kirk) [M1; P1]
> There is a hunter hunting for animals (Abbi) [M1; P1]
> People put music on inside the house and left the doors wide open to be able to hear it outside (Charlotte) [M2; P1]
> Someone is jumping in the water happily (Harry) [M2; P1]
> Someone is playing an instrument, like a violin, in the house with the window open (Sheila) [M2; P1]
> Some people are crossing the bridge (Ellie) [M2; P1]
> Ellie and Charlotte are crossing the bridge, looking at their reflection (Abbi) [M2; P1]
> Someone died: they fell off the bridge, fell into the water (Carl) [M2; P1]
> A whale jumped up there (Kirk) [M2; P1]
> It is night and it is like an owl whistling (Josh) [M1; P2]
> The village is haunted ... the bushes swing in the wind and the crickets are noisy (Nathan) [M1; P2]

These Year 2 children applied a number of cognitive strategies for interpreting musical experience, and seemed to be able to move fluently between these strategies Most seemed to be aware of the musical conventions that ascribe an anxious or scary character to one piece of music and a bright, happy character to the other piece, and used this latent knowledge to construct musical meaning in a visual context. Some identified specific elements of the music and related these to the detail of the pictures. Children built on others' ideas to refine their own interpretation. The juxtaposition of the two kinds of stimuli appear to have focused children's attention on both and enhanced their ability to articulate their experience of the stimuli.

Some children used musical vocabulary, but most children constructed their own way of expressing musical (and pictorial) meaning, unhindered by the absence of such vocabulary. However, the next stage in their development could well be moving towards a more specific and professional vocabulary by investigating the components of the musical meanings they have identified.

What is music?

Play a musical stimulus of a problematical nature, such as African or jazz drumming, rap, nature sounds (including birdsong or whale sounds), or a twentieth-century composition that does not fulfil the conventional expectations of melody and/or harmony. Ask the children to make up questions about it, or ask them yourself whether what they heard was music or not, and why or why not.

In order to answer the question of whether the stimulus counts as music, or not, the children need to establish criteria for regarding something as music. As they embark on this, they are likely to find that they have different understandings of what constitutes music, often depending on their cultural or ethnic backgrounds. A shared definition of music, therefore, has to be negotiated, and all arguments need to be supported by reasoning. In the process children can be helped to consider musical concepts like pitch, rhythm, tune, accompaniment, musical sounds and noise, accidental and deliberate (composed) musical sounds, music as communication or as a language, the role of the composer and the listener, and possibly also the place of music in society and the role of the music industry. Such discussions can touch on aspects of music theory, musical perception or the psychology of music as well as the philosophy and sociology of music. All groups of pupils, from Year 2 to Year 10 that I have worked with have shown interest and enthusiasm for such discussions.

What animal could it be?

Play a movement from Camille Saint-Saens's *The Carnival of the Animals* without revealing the movement's title. Ask children to suggest what type of animal the music might be describing. What elements of the music support the idea of that animal? What type of animal could it definitely not be about? Encourage and help children to use musical vocabulary as much as possible but don't make it a condition of contribution.

The purpose is not to guess the animal that is depicted in the music – although it is very rewarding if it happens – but to give the best possible (i.e. the most articulate, accurate and detailed) reasons for choosing a particular animal. Emphasise that there is not one right answer, only better and less good reasoning to support a particular conclusion.

Examples from Year 1 and Year 6

Children use musical vocabulary and reasoning after listening to 'The Swan'.

D:	I think a rabbit is one.
Facilitator (F):	Why?
D:	Because it goes up and down.
F:	How does that connect with the rabbit?
D:	The violin is going down and the piano is going down and then it starts going back up, like it's getting all louder.

F:	You are absolutely right about all that, but how is that like a rabbit? Can you explain the connection?
D:	Shall I show you? (walks about with heavy steps)
F:	Is that the going up and going down again?
D:	Yes.

Year 6

B:	I thought it was a foreign place, like a rainforest – lots of water and hot and wet atmosphere, from the long bowing on the cello.
F:	How does that relate to the rainforest? The long bowing?
B:	It made me think of a snake.
D:	I thought it was an animal dying.
F:	Why?
D:	It's sad and slow music.
J:	I said it was graceful. It could have been a swan because they are very graceful, it gave me the impression that it was up, flying in the air, then came down and landed on the water.
F:	What in the music gave you that?
J:	It was going higher, the notes higher, then lower. And it was very slow . . . I just thought of another reason why it might be a swan. The notes, they all slur together, it's not all short. I don't agree with K that it is a hopping animal. I don't think that's the type of music it is.
F:	Can anyone think of the musical term for what J was describing, when the notes are connected up together?
J:	Legato. And it is not staccato, because that is jumpy, chopped up.
F:	Would you say that K's image is more a staccato image?
J:	Yes.

This session was helpful for clarifying musical concepts and building a musical vocabulary, by relating something extra-musical, i.e. animals, to a musical stimulus. As even young children know a great deal about animals, they feel motivated enough to battle with expressing the connections they perceive between the music and their chosen animal. The children in Year 6 were able to give extended interpretations based on their wider experience of life.

Conclusion

This chapter has argued that the arts curriculum should involve not only 'making and doing' but also 'talking about' music, art and design. The reservoirs of hidden knowledge that children have got can be activated through the process of aesthetic enquiry. Children can be creatively engaged with big questions about the arts. They can be supported in developing their artistic tastes and empowered to participate creatively and actively in aesthetic enquiry through posing and responding to questions relating to art or music.

A number of practical examples have been offered to show how the 'community of enquiry' approach provides a format for successful group discussion. A community of enquiry can be a truly democratic place of learning where children learn to pose, and collaborate in finding answers to questions of their own choosing. The stimulus to aesthetic enquiry can be pieces of music, paintings, photographs, sculpture, craftwork, a design, an edifice, a dance, drama or mime. Aesthetic enquiry can investigate objects or genres that do not necessarily fall into the conventional aesthetic categories, such as adverts, product catalogues, 'found objects', fragments or children's own work. The philosophical dimensions of artistic experience can be opened up by scrutinising assumptions that underlie the assessment of any work.

A number of starting points have been suggested, including games, which can be used to stimulate creative thinking and response to aesthetic questions. Through discussion children can be helped to clarify concepts and an aesthetic vocabulary. The 'collaborative conversations' that take place in a community of enquiry can be a source of effective and sustained learning for children in and through the arts. Such discussion, whether it takes place before or after 'making and doing', enables children to move between verbal and non-verbal modes of expression and meaning-making. It helps them to articulate and develop their own thinking and to benefit from the thinking of others. In so doing they become critical thinkers about music and art and also about their culture and communities.

Notes

1   Andersson, Liptai, Sutton and Williams (2003) *Ta(l)king Pictures: Thinking Through Photographs* (Birmingham: Imaginative Minds) provides a useful resource and teacher's manual drawing on material from an aesthetic enquiry and art project, focusing on the use of scanners, photography and photographic techniques in art education and offering a step-by-step guide to aesthetic enquiry. It includes laminated A4 images and CD-ROM with printable images of art work by children and adults and is suitable for children in Key Stages 2 and 3.

2   See also *Teaching Thinking* by Robert Fisher (2003) for a classic introduction to *Philosophy for Children*, especially suitable for Key Stage 2 teachers. Chapter 7, 'Philosophy across the curriculum', contains sections on art and music. Haynes (2002) offers a comprehensive yet easy-to-read introduction, consistently making the arguments through children's voices, and locates *Philosophy for Children* within the current educational and political context. It includes many examples of work with pupils in the early years of education.

3   This game is adapted from Robert Fisher's *Games for Thinking* (1997), pp. 135–6.

Further reading

Andersson A., Liptai, S., Sutton R. and Williams S. (2003) *Ta(l)king Pictures: Thinking Through Photographs.* Birmingham: Imaginative Minds.

Fisher, R (2003) *Teaching Thinking: Philosophical Enquiry in the Classroom*, London: Continuum.

Haynes, J (2002) *Children as Philosophers: Learning through Enquiry and Dialogue in the Primary Classroom.* London: Routledge.

Creativity through religious education

Lynne Broadbent

'Religious education . . . [will] gain a more profound understanding of itself by listening to the questions which the expressive arts raise.'

(Derek Webster 1982)

THIS CHAPTER EXPLORES THE concept of creativity in relation to religion and its contribution to pupils' religious education and spiritual development. It draws upon current theories and approaches to religious education and is supported by reference to classroom practice.

Creativity – in religion?

Religions are dynamic and life-changing; they are about revelation and inspiration, with the lives of key figures, such as Moses, transformed through encounters with the divine in a burning bush and new communities formed from a disparate collection of persecuted slaves. Religions, therefore, could be regarded as synonymous with creativity because they are about change and movement, about making something new. This is not an image readily associated with religion. So what *is* religion?

Brainstorming the word 'religion' with groups of students, teachers and even clergy usually elicits authoritarian and negative words and connotations. Religions are commonly perceived as being concerned with lists of laws and rules and requiring conformity from their followers. But this is not borne out by study of the history of religions, where the key figures were rarely conformist and were frequently the very people who challenged the laws and customs of the cultures in which they lived – this would be true of Jesus, the Prophet Muhammad, the Buddha and Guru Nanak. They rarely provided slick and simplistic rules for daily living but, rather, demanded that their followers reflect on their present way of life, respond to the challenge of change and live life according to a new vision. This is also true for individual believers today who engage with the stories and rituals of their religious tradition and find their eyes and minds opened to new ways of living, and for whole communities who are challenged as to how to apply their religious teachings to situations of war, the inclusion of homosexuals in the priesthood and the concept of forgiveness and neighbourliness in a global community.

Religions themselves draw upon art and architecture as outward expressions of inner beliefs, and, at times, as an evocation to worship. The openness of the space within a mosque, for example, often coupled with the harmony of geometric shapes and Arabic script, contributes to an atmosphere of meditation and prayer, while the design of a Hindu temple, or mandir, often incorporating a representation of the Himalayas where the gods traditionally resided, symbolises a meeting place between the worshipper and the divine. For Eastern Orthodox Christians, icons of saints provide 'windows to the divine' and are a focus for prayers of intercession. In other Christian churches, stained-glass windows and religious paintings were, historically, a means of passing on biblical stories and teachings to those who could not read them for themselves. Aslet (1991) identifies a further role of Christian art when he speaks of an individual entering a church, a 'sacred space': 'through art he or she could enter sacred time. Art was a means by which people could transcend this world and their own suffering.'

There is therefore an intrinsic relationship between religion and creativity, the relationship operating at many different levels. Revelations generate new philosophies and ways of living; architecture both reflects and inspires distinctive beliefs and forms of worship while painting and even religious music explain and express the artist's and composer's inner commitments in varied forms. They certainly verify Ken Robinson's definition of creativity, quoted by Fisher in Chapter 1, as 'imaginative processes with outcomes that are original and of value'. So this raises the question as to how the relationship between religion and creativity might be translated into religious education in the classroom. Are we to transform our pupils into creative thinkers, artists and performers, or into objective observers of the creative arts? And how do we do this while preserving the integrity of the art itself, for while our teaching intentions might be focused on learning in religious education, for the artist the art is art in its own right; it was not created to serve as an illustration for a particular teaching point.

How does religious education contribute to creativity and vice versa?

Any creative approaches used in Religious Education need to contribute to the subject's core aims: first, of developing knowledge and understanding of religions and their influence on the lives of individuals and communities. This relates to one of the two common aims for religious education, namely 'learning about religions'. But religious education is more than the development of knowledge and understanding – for the second aim, or attainment target, 'learning from religion', presents pupils with opportunities to respond to what they have learned about religion and relate it to their own lives. This introduces a personal dimension to learning in religious education, although this is not related in any way to nurturing, persuading or indoctrinating pupils into belief itself – which is certainly not part of an educational aim and, indeed, not allowed by law. This personal dimension means engaging pupils with religious material, for example religious stories, people, places and teachings, and enabling them to relate these features of religious experience to common human experiences. Such a process demands that pupils develop skills, for example the skill of *reflection*, of thinking through what one has seen or experienced; of *interpretation*, of suggesting meaning for, say, symbols or actions; of *empathetic imagination*, of appreciating what the experience might mean to the believer or even non-believer; and of *application*, applying what one has learned to new situations, whether religious or part of everyday human experience. Together, these skills harness both the mind and the emotions and lend themselves to intellectual and creative forms of expression. It may be argued, therefore, that the interface between attainment targets 1 and 2, of 'learning about religions' and 'learning from religion', readily lends itself to creativity in the classroom. So how might this be planned in practice?

Creativity through the use of story

Religions transmit their beliefs, values and traditions to new generations of believers, largely through the telling of stories. Some stories about key figures or events in the history of the community are retold annually at festival times, others are recounted in weekly sermons and by parents and grandparents to children and grandchildren. Storytelling is thus a powerful medium for believers to learn about their religion, and to learn from the story how they should behave and respond as part of a religious family or community. The story serves as a mirror to one's life, both as an individual and as a member of a community. The question is, can stories be used in the classroom to enable pupils to learn about religion and to serve as a mirror to their own lives, albeit from a human rather than religious perspective? Furthermore, could such a process be deemed to be 'creative'? On hearing stories in religious education pupils frequently ask, 'Is it true, Miss?' It is a very good question to ask, for it makes us reflect upon our own lives to see whether there is anything in our past or present experience which resonates with the themes of the story. But this question should then be followed by a second question, asking 'Who am I?' or 'Where do I stand in the story?' Then the story becomes a mirror for our own experience.

Using story with students: an example

In a session with a group of students training for primary teaching, we considered how children frequently ask, 'Is it true, Miss?' and questioned what we mean by 'true' in storytelling. We read the story of *Dogger* (Hughes 1979) and asked whether it was true. Well, certainly it was; there might not have been a Dave or a stuffed toy dog named Dogger, but we all knew just how Dave felt when he thought he had lost Dogger for good – we had all experienced sleepless hours at the pain of loss, maybe of a beloved toy or of a person; so yes, it was true. Then we read *Angry Arthur* (Oram 1993) and immediately related to how angry Arthur had become when his desire to stay up late was thwarted by his parents; so indeed it was true. But then we turned our attention to the story of Adam and Eve in a spectacular garden with the fruit of one tree forbidden and tempted to taste fruit from that very tree. Was it true? Most students were silent: it seemed to them inappropriate to ask this question of religious text. We swiftly addressed a second question: 'Have you ever felt like Adam and Eve, tempted to do the very thing you know you shouldn't do?' Instantly they responded, the text no longer being too 'sacred' to question but acting as a mirror through which they were able to reflect upon and interpret their own lives and human experiences. This is how believers use the text, following on with the question 'What should I do and how should I behave, in the light of my beliefs?'

For those of other faith traditions, or of none, the question might be, 'What should I do in the light of my beliefs about the world, or my personal values?' This is creative activity for we are reinterpreting our experiences anew in the light of the story we have heard, and in so doing the process becomes part of our personal development, whether we are believers or not. Furthermore, by approaching most religious stories in this way we are being true to the original intentions of the text. David Jasper (1991) contends that for too long the Bible has not been actually read either within or outside the religious traditions, but rather people have had the stories read to them and have simply accepted the interpretation of the reader. This is frequently what happens in school where teaching is restricted to an approach based on 'This is a religious story and this is what it means'.

Using story in the classroom: an example

A Year 5 class had listened to the story of the Prodigal, or Lost Son, the story of the younger son asking his father for his share of his inheritance, leaving home and spending the money on having a good time. When the money runs out and the son is forced to share the food given to pigs, he decides to go home and ask his father's forgiveness. His father accepts him back and incites the elder brother's jealousy when he throws a party for the younger son. The pupils were invited to brainstorm in groups the questions they would like to ask any or each of the characters in the story. The questions were shared and a few were selected by the pupils as the basis for class discussion; these questions included asking the younger brother whether he was truly sorry, the father whether he could trust his son again and the brother whether he continued to feel jealous the following day. The discussion enabled the pupils to engage with the characters, tease out motivations and reflect upon behaviours and attitudes. Then came the big question – 'Who, in the story, are you most like?' This was a real test of empathetic imagination and application, not to mention honesty.

Some weeks later, this story and approach were used again but with a class of Year 9 pupils in a secondary school. They remembered hearing the story at primary school and agreed, patiently, to hear it again. This time the group brainstorming activity sparked loud debate and dissension and the 'audacity' of the resulting questions surprised many in the class; for example, the father was asked, 'What kind of father was he to give his son the money in the first place?' and 'How could his elder son ever feel confident in his fairness again?' Pupils were silenced by the question, 'Who in the story were they, or would they be, most like?' They left the classroom baffled by an explanation of the Christian context of the story, that the father, in his giving of the money and in his forgiveness, is an analogy for God. Lealman (1982) refers to the sense of paradox in religion where questions 'only produce other questions and cannot find satisfaction in simple solutions and certainties'. Bausch's description of the creative power of story (1984) was certainly reflected in the reaction of the pupils. He suggests that:

> [when the story] has gotten inside of you, it has a life of its own (even when you've done with it, it is not done with you) and it kind of rinses through you. You can't put into words what the effect is, but there is a resonance, perhaps even a free-floating disturbance.

This creative approach to the use of story in religious education demands reflection and interpretation and generates new ways of seeing it could be used effectively with most, but not all, religious stories. A cautionary note would apply predominantly to Muslim stories about the Prophet Muhammad and to Sikh stories involving the Gurus. First, it would not be appropriate in Muslim tradition to question or interpret the intentions of the Prophet, neither would it be appropriate to role play or 'hot seat' the Prophet. So, for example, in the story of the Prophet and the Old Woman who constantly threw rubbish at the Prophet as he walked in the street, it would not be appropriate to ask what the Prophet thought on the day when no rubbish was thrown, or why he went to investigate what had happened to the woman, although it would be possible to interrogate the old woman and ask what she felt when the Prophet visited and helped her, when he discovered that she was ill. Similarly, it would not be acceptable to role play the Gurus in Sikhism, so in the story of Bhai Kaneeya, the Water Carrier, who after a day's battle gives water to all the wounded, Sikh and non-Sikh, and is subsequently criticised by his fellow soldiers, we could hear the arguments of the soldiers and Bhai Kaneeya's response, but the Guru's speech in support of Bhai Kaneeya would have to be by reportage rather than role play. But beyond these few, yet significant, notes of caution, we should be as creative as possible when using story as a basis for reflective questioning.

. . . and the expressive arts?

Derek Webster (1982) states that 'Religious education will not sanctify the arts by employing them as so many puppets to dance for itself. It will, however, gain a more profound understanding of itself by listening to the questions which the expressive arts raise.' Any selection of paintings depicting Jesus' birth, life and crucifixion will reflect a wide diversity of image and expression, each painting presenting the artist's interpretation of a particular event and each painting now having a life of its own. Martland (quoted Starkings 1993) speaking of Leonardo's painting *The Last Supper*, states: 'It is not about the last supper: rather the painting itself is the actual "Last Supper"; that is, it presents to the world a new understanding of that supper event'. Similarly, Stanley Spencer's painting, *Resurrection of the People of Cookham*, with its very modern, and often very amusing, characters crawling out of graves and tombs, raises for us questions about the concept of resurrection.

The creative use of paintings and images: a scenario

A class of Year 5 pupils is approaching the Christian festival of Easter through studying paintings of the Crucifixion. The pupils are working in small groups, each group using one of the paintings and asking what the artist was trying to show in his or her work. It is evident that the task is raising many questions within each group. In the whole-class feedback one of the girls asks: 'Why did they nail Jesus when the other two men [on the crosses] are only tied?' The question is thrown open to the rest of the class and the pupils attempt to imaginatively enter the world of the artist's interpretation, posing questions and postulating answers while drawing upon their knowledge of the political and religious situations leading to Jesus' death. The stimulus is an art-based activity but in the process learning in religious education is deepened.

Starkings (1991) suggests that asking and exploring questions is a teaching method which gives priority to personal discovery, and cites an example of work undertaken by a group of 10–12-year-olds on the Buddha rupa or image. The aim was to see whether Buddhist values and teachings could be grasped *experientially* through use of art. The pupils were shown a large poster of a seated Buddha rupa and were told that this was not a photograph of the Buddha but a statue or image which had been made to illustrate important qualities of the Buddha. They were then asked whether words were always needed to understand what someone was thinking or feeling. To prompt pupils' thinking, the teacher sat with his feet resting on the desk, hands behind his head, silently whistling! The pupils gradually got the idea and began to make links between the outer signs of bodily posture and the inner thoughts or feelings which might be reflected through them. Attention then turned to the Buddha rupa, his 'calm' posture and his slightly lowered eyelids suggesting that the Buddha was looking inwards, 'watching his own thoughts'. The teacher encouraged the pupils to consider what the Buddha noticed when he watched his own thoughts. With the help of carefully considered questioning, they began to notice the world around them: the sun, the clouds racing across the sky and the trees in bloom – all things which change constantly. Nothing in the world stays the same. They applied this principle to themselves and their feelings – to feelings of joy, sadness and fear – and were invited to draw, paint or write, in poetry or prose, examples of 'before' and 'after', the natural process of change in the world. The resulting pieces of creativity were displayed around the picture of the Buddha.

Art – specifically a Buddha rupa – had challenged pupils' understanding of Buddhist teachings and meditation and given rise to pupils' creative responses. This example highlights clearly the parallel processes of 'learning about religions' and 'learning from religion' and demonstrates the development of creative thinking skills, i.e. of reflection, interpretation and application. A similar approach could be used with Hindu images of God, or with the pictures, life and teaching of Guru Nanak, the first of the ten Sikh gurus, whose bodily posture reflects his spiritual nature and his meditation on the name of god, while McGinty (1991) identifies a project undertaken with a group of 15-year-olds following a visit to the Tate Gallery in Liverpool to see an exhibition of sculptures entitled 'Images of Life'. The pupils studied and sketched, and, in small groups, discussed the emotions generated by the sculptures. This elicited a wide range of responses, from sadness and oppression to elation and freedom, and these responses were expressed through poetry, body sculpture, dance and drama, incorporating topics such as abortion, civil rights, the strength of God's love and the plight of the disabled in today's society – all topics which might form part of a GCSE course on Religion and Society.

Music is another medium which both reflects and evokes powerful emotions: the vivaciousness of gospel rhythms, the meditative quality of Taizé chants, the echoes of the Call to Prayer coming from a minaret and the haunting quality of the Kol Nidre heard in the synagogue at Yom Kippur, the Jewish Day of Atonement. Pupils are being creative when they are listening to and responding, or composing and performing, music related to religious traditions.

The creative use of music: an example

A class of Year 5 and 6 pupils from a local school visited Canterbury Cathedral, their task to experience the atmosphere and to notice the sounds in different parts of the building on that day. Back at school, using a range of traditional instruments, including the human voice and synthesisers, the pupils set to work, creating their experiences in musical composition. Their compositions incorporated both the silence and quiet recitation of prayer, the stillness of thoughtful reflection, the echoes of the lofty building, the bustle of visitors, the dramatic clashes of murder, the Cathedral being the site of the murder of Thomas Becket, and the singing of well-known hymns. The resulting performances certainly illustrated that the pupils had engaged their empathy and imagination and had developed skills of reflection and interpretation, while the project itself had combined religious education with history and music. As well as religious buildings being a source of inspiration for composition, religious stories and life-cycle events, such as birth, coming of age, marriage and death, can provide a stimulus. Other studies have focused on comparing the different traditions of religious words and music. For example, in one school, pupils studied the Psalms and their musical settings with some of Bob Marley's music, in particular his *Redemption Song*.

Music can also be composed to support dramatic presentations on religious themes. Teachers are adept at incorporating the dramatic role play of stories, such as the Lost Son, and dilemmas such as Sikh boys or girls who displease their parents by wanting to cut their hair, but the recent increase in films based on biblical stories opens the way for extensive creative work in the classroom. The Testament series, which includes the stories of Abraham, Moses and Ruth, the film *Moses, Prince of Egypt*, and, more recently, *The Miracle Maker*, all rely on music to highlight the key action taking place on screen. In the Testament version of the story of Moses, for example, music becomes the means of conveying the presence and movement of the Angel of Death the night before the Hebrews escaped from slavery. Using these films as models, pupils could make films of other religious stories and events, writing character sketches and stage notes and solving 'religious' problems as to how events such as revelations, visitations by angels and characters such as the Prophet Muhammad, who cannot be illustrated, might be conveyed on screen. Not only do these strategies engage pupils in the subject or theme of the story but they themselves become artists, interpreting the story anew in similar mode to the classical painter.

The creative use of drama: an example

Writing about the contribution of religious education to pupils' spiritual development, Hammond (2002) cites two examples of dramatic presentation. The first, frequently linked to religious perspectives on the environment, is *The Council of All Beings*. Pupils begin by reflecting on situations in the natural world which bring them joy and those which bring sadness; having discussed their responses in silence, they identify a facet of nature for which they feel a particular attraction – an animal, tree, plant, mountain or river. They then make masks to represent their selected item. The Council assembles to the sound of music or drumming, and, following some readings, each 'being' speaks of their life and struggle, concluding with a message for the 'two-legged ones'. When all have spoken, the masks are removed and placed in a circle, and the participants, the 'two-legged ones', take what they have heard back into their daily lives.

Hammond's second example comes from the work of Sue Phillips (1999) and her enactment of Yom Kippur, the Jewish Day of Atonement, with its themes of repentance and renewal, with a group of secondary students. The classroom was set out like a synagogue and draped in white; the students entered to the sound of Kol Nidre. After listening to traditional readings, the students thought of their own regrets and imagined putting these regrets into a stone, which was then placed in a bowl of water for symbolic cleansing. During the debriefing, one of the students commented, 'It's alright for the Jews, they do it every year. I had so much to regret in a whole lifetime.' Both events were rituals which, like most rituals, harnessed both intellectual and emotional experiences. As earlier examples, they interwove learning about religions and learning from religion, raising personal and universal questions in challenging and creative enactments.

What are the implications of a creative approach to learning in religious education?

The NACCCE Report (1999) recognised that 'promoting creative and cultural education is not a simple matter. It will involve a gradual review of the styles, purposes and ethos of education at many levels.' Certainly in an era where creativity has been sacrificed in the face of an overriding concern for tightly prescriptive programmes of study and for regular and rigorous assessment, there is a need to consider the implications for teachers, pupils and the curriculum as a whole. In Chapter 1, Fisher suggests that 'effective learners need creative teachers who provide both order and adventure, who are willing to do the unexpected and to take risks'. The approaches to learning identified above are indeed risky; they do not require from pupils slick and simplistic answers to sets of questions, but rather they seek to challenge pupils' thinking and stimulate diverse responses – and diversity can feel dangerous.

In religious education a creative approach to learning requires a teacher who has a good grasp of the subject and feels sufficiently confident to encourage pupils to engage in exploration and interpretation of its meaning. Having a good grasp of the subject is a tall order, for religious education is a territory that encompasses six major religions. It does not mean we need to know all there is to know about each religion, but, in the words of the NACCCE Report, having 'a growing understanding of the possibilities, range and methods'. A teacher who does not feel confident and competent is likely to restrict themselves to tried, tested and predictable teaching strategies and is unlikely to venture into the often unknown waters of creativity. But if it is true that religions, in essence, are dynamic, and are about change and creativity, then to teach about them in ways devoid of creativity is to misrepresent the nature of the subject.

Creative approaches to teaching can engage and stimulate all pupils, encouraging their active involvement with the subject matter, including the stories, the paintings and the music. Religions are not just for the bright and the beautiful, they are for all. Religions are multi-dimensional and use visual image, sounds, smells and touch to convey message and meaning, and this should be reflected in the religious education classroom. A glance at the QCA (2000) guidance for teaching RE reveals frequent reference to the need for pupils to 'respond to' or 'suggest meanings or answers for', indicating personal engagement in reflection, empathetic imagination, interpretation and application, all skills emanating from a creative approach to learning. This raises the further question of whether the curriculum and syllabuses for religious education are too content-laden. Many teachers find that the ever-increasing abundance of what should be learned and understood is mind-blowing. Moreover, syllabus content is frequently fragmented into sections such as beliefs, worship and rites of passage, and unrelated to the holistic way a believer experiences their faith. How then do we ensure that pupils have the opportunity to make sense of religious questions and experiences and their importance in the lives of people throughout the world?

Phenix (1964) considered that education was a process of engendering essential meanings and that one of the threats to meaning-making was the volume of knowledge to be learned. A religious education without meaning-making would result in a programme of sociological fact-gathering. We need, therefore, to undertake a review of the amount of knowledge to be learned and the quality of the learning which is to take place, and to reinstate an approach to teaching and learning in religious education that harnesses the creativity of teachers, pupils and syllabus constructors.

So, creativity through religious education? It is possible, challenging, and necessary.

Further reading

Aslet, C. (1991) 'The Isenheim Altarpiece', in *RE and the Creative Arts*. The Shap Working Party on World Religions.

Bausch, W.J. (1984) *Storytelling, Imagination and Faith*. Connecticut: Twenty-Third Publications.

Hammond, J. (2002) 'Embodying the spirit: realising RE's potential in the spiritual dimension of the curriculum', in Broadbent, L. and Brown A. (eds) *Issues in Religious Education*: London: RoutledgeFalmer.

Jasper, D. (1991), 'How can we read the Bible?', in Gearon, L. (1999) *Literature, Theology and the Curriculum*. London: Cassell.

Lealman, B. (1982) 'Blue wind and broken image', in *Religious Education and the Imagination: Aspects of Education*. University of Hull.

McGinty, S. (1991) 'Religion and the arts', in *RE and the Creative Arts*. Shap Working Party on World Religions in Education.

NACCCE (1999) *All Our Futures: Creativity, Culture and Education*. National Advisory Committee on Creative and Cultural Education Report. London: DfEE.

Phenix, P.H. (1964) *Realms of Meaning*. McGraw-Hill: New York.

Phillips, S. (1999) 'Experiential learning', in *Can I Teach Your Religion?* The Shap Working Party on World Religions in Education.

QCA (2000) *Religious Education: Non-statutory Guidance on RE*. London: QCA.

Starkings, D. (1991) 'The Buddha: images and ideas': in *RE and the Creative Arts*: The Shap Working Party on World Religions in Education.

Starkings, D. (1993) 'The landscape of spirituality', in Starkings, D. (ed.) *Religion and the Arts in Education: Dimensions of Spirituality*. Sevenoaks: Hodder & Stoughton.

Webster, D.H. (1982) 'Spiritual growth in religious education', in *Religious Education and the Imagination: Aspects of Education*. University of Hull.

Children's literature

Hughes, Shirley (1979) *Dogger*. London: Collins Picture Lions.

Oram, Hiawyn (1993) *Angry Arthur*. London: Red Fox.

12

Creativity across the curriculum

Robert Fisher

'I knew the work would be a challenge but I have now learned that I can do anything if I put my mind to it.'

(Katie, aged 10)

CHILDREN LIKE KATIE NEED opportunities, but they also need the confidence to be creative. Her teachers also need the confidence to take risks and to engage pupils in open-ended tasks that challenge them not just to do but also to think and create in new ways. Her school also needs the courage to cut down on the content of the curriculum to allow more time for the creative curriculum. In reviewing progress in creativity a school needs to think about its commitment to promoting creativity and how it is expressed in different subject areas across the curriculum. This chapter reviews the concept of creativity, identifies a range of teaching strategies that can be used to foster it across the curriculum and presents two case studies showing how creativity is being implemented in schools.

Reviewing creativity

Questions to discuss when reviewing creativity in school might include:

- Does our school have a commitment to promoting creativity?
- What is our concept of creativity?
- How is it expressed in different subject areas?

(For further questions to discuss in reviewing creativity in school, see Appendix.)

By creativity we mean forms of thinking that develop young people's capacity for original ideas and action. There are many misconceptions about creativity. Some people only associate it with the arts, or particular types of individual, or think it cannot be taught or nurtured. Our concept of creative thinking recognises the potential for creative thinking in all fields of human activity, and that all have the capacity for such achievements.

Creative thinking is shown when children generate outcomes, show imagination and originality and can judge the value of what they have done. What promotes creativity is a questioning classroom where teachers and pupils ask unusual and challenging questions; where new connections are made; where ideas are represented in different ways – visually, physically and verbally; where there are fresh approaches and solutions to problems; and where the effects of ideas and actions are critically evaluated.

Creative thinking is not a single power but is multi-dimensional. Creative thinking develops through practice and involves:

- creative use of the techniques, skills and processs of a subject discipline; and
- use of general features of creative thinking that apply across all subject areas such as brainstorming, mindmapping, imagination, visualisation and lateral thinking.

Creative thinking is a basic capacity of human intelligence. The ability of our pupils to represent their experience in various ways is fundamental to how they think, communicate and view themselves. They are able to think about the world in the ways they experience it – through words, visually, in sound, in movement and so on. They experience it through social interaction and personal reflection. Conventional education tends to emphasise verbal and mathematical reasoning. These are vital but they are not the whole of intelligence, and they, too, need to be developed through creative thinking.

The multi-faceted nature of human intelligence has three important implications for education. First, it is not accurate or possible to judge children's intelligence on academic ability alone. Secondly, children who, for whatever reason, perform poorly in conventional academic tests may have strong abilities in other areas, including creative thinking. Thirdly, all pupils can develop creativity through different modes of learning.

Creative thinking focuses on 'knowing how' as well as 'knowing what'. The National Curriculum (2000) recognises creative thinking as one of the key skills in thinking and in learning. These skills are embedded in all subjects and enable pupils to:

- generate and extend ideas;
- suggest hypotheses;
- apply imagination;
- consider things from alternative viewpoints; and
- look for alternative outcomes.

Any lesson can develop creative thinking if it involves pupils generating and extending ideas, suggesting hypotheses, applying imagination and finding new or innovative outcomes. How is creativity to be fostered in the lessons you teach?

Teaching strategies

The following teaching strategies can be applied to a wide range of curriculum areas to encourage pupils to apply imagination, generate and extend ideas, suggest hypotheses, look for alternative innovative outcomes and exercise their critical judgement.

Use imagination

Think of new ideas, speculate on what might be possible and apply imagination to improve outcomes. Question cues might include:

- What might happen if . . . (if not)?
- Design a new way to . . .
- Suggest an improvement on . . .

Generate more ideas

Generate many responses, encourage thinking of alternatives and greater fluency of ideas. Question cues could be:

- How many kinds of . . . can you think of?
- List all . . . that could be used for . . .?
- What might be the arguments for . . . (and against)?

Experiment with alternatives

Be willing to change one's initial ideas, see things another way, experiment with alternative approaches.
  Question cues:

- How else might you . . .?
- Think of five ways of/questions to ask about/reasons for . . .
- List ten things you could do with . . . (a shape, recipe, piece of music, picture, object, design brief, photo, news story etc.)

Be original

Think of novel ideas, unique solutions, and design original plans.
  Question cues:

- Design a game for . . .
- Invent a way to . . .
- Think of a way to improve . . . (an object, game, text, plan etc.)

Expand on what we do and know

Elaborate on what you know, build on a given situation, make it more interesting.
Question cues:

- What might we add . . . (e.g. to a story, picture, design)
- What might we change . . . (e.g. to make it different, more interesting)
- What is another way to . . . (e.g. solve a problem, apply an algorithm, investigate a hypothesis)

Assess what we have thought and done

Evaluate the creative process and judge the outcome.
Question cues:

- What criteria should we use to judge whether . . .?
- What is good/could be improved/is interesting about . . .
- What could/should you/we do next . . .?

If pupils are to develop their creativity they need creative teachers, and teachers need to work in schools where creativity is valued and shared. What is your vision of a creative school?

Creative schools

Schools need the courage to be creative, and to put creativity at the heart of the curriculum. The following are case studies of two schools that are focusing on ways to develop creativity across the curriculum.

Case Study 1: Westbury Park School, Bristol

Four years ago Bristol LEA invested much time, energy and money in the 'Flying High' project, aimed at meeting the needs of able children. Many involved in the project soon realised that activities designed to meet the needs of 'high fliers' would also meet the needs of all children as well as stretching the gifted and talented. They realised, in the words of Westbury Park's head teacher, Alan Rees, that they needed 'HOTS not MOTS – Higher Order Thinking Skills not More Of The Same'.

Westbury Park Primary School has found that a focus on thinking skills can have a dramatic effect on the way the school works to maximise the learning of children. 'Thinking skills has had a huge impact on the school,' says Alan Rees, 'as we escape from under the thumb of the National Curriculum, use Literacy and Numeracy strategies more flexibly and focus on helping children to become effective and lifelong learners.'

The school believes that a focus on creative thinking skills adds value to the vision. 'Thinking skills have helped teachers to teach the National Curriculum in more purposeful and creative ways,' says Alan Rees, 'providing the children with more exciting and stimulating classrooms, so that both staff and children are more motivated to learn.'

As in any school the role of middle management has been crucial to the success of policy innovations. Marcelo Staricoff, leader of the school's thinking skills curriculum, co-ordinates many of the current initiatives. Current initiatives aimed at using thinking skills approaches to transform learning include:

- developing the thinking environment of the classroom;
- philosophy for children;
- thinking science;
- more flexible literacy and numeracy hours; and
- leading CPD on thinking skills techniques in school and LEA.

Evidence of a thinking school is to be found in thinking classrooms.

Thinking classrooms

'There is so much to look at and think about' (Y5 pupil)

Year 5 class teacher Marcelo believes that the children need to feel they are working within a Thinking Classroom. Part of his whiteboard is dedicated to the daily thinking skills challenge as well as a daily dose of Spanish, news items and relevant websites. This creates a sense of expectation as the children come into the classroom each morning, which, as class member Kate says, is 'very stimulating'. There is a permanent display showing key words about learning styles and thinking skills. Evidence of specific techniques is displayed, such as 'Mind Mapping' (tree diagrams showing connections between ideas), 'PMI' (listing the Plus, Minus and Interesting points of a topic) or 'concept cartoons' created by the children. A table of 'thinking books' and resources is freely available for children to consult.

As the children enter the class they are greeted with classical music and a thinking challenge, which might be a verbal, mathematical or visual puzzle; a problem, investigation or challenge such as working out the similarities and differences between ketchup and blood. They tackle the daily task in their A4-size Thinking Books, which is then shared in class but not marked. Children find these 'thinking starters' to the day a good preparation for the lessons ahead. As pupil Georgie put it, 'I think I am most creative in the morning because when I think deeply it gets my mind working for the rest of the day'.

Thinking time is built in before lessons when they think about and describe the learning objective (TLP or Today's Learning Point); during lessons when the teacher tries to include a thinking skills enrichment task intended to motivate the children to apply in a different context or explain a key concept to a partner; and at the end when children think about and add a TIL (Today I Learnt) point to their work. Children are also encouraged to think about their thinking (metacognition). Kate, aged 10, for example, wrote that thinking skills for her is creativity 'as a different word'.

Time for creativity

Time for creativity is built into each day. For example, each afternoon begins with an 'Artistic Performance', in which children are invited to share something they have created, such as music, a play, song, dance, poem, story, improvisational game, magic or even juggling. Marcelo comments that 'these sessions create a very positive and relaxed atmosphere and set the tone for the rest of the afternoon. They provide children with opportunities for creative expression that might otherwise not fit into a busy curriculum'. They give them, says Marcelo, 'time to shine'. As one of the children commented, 'Other children really inspire me to perform'.

The school has had an Artsmark audit and is implementing a creativity policy with a number of creative targets, including offering every child the opportunity to learn the recorder, involving more boys in arts activities and having cultural focus days such as Asian Arts day. Creative experience and enjoyment are ensured through a planned programme of visits and performances. But creativity is not seen as something belonging only to the traditional arts, vital though these are. The school seeks to build creativity into all curriculum areas. This is expressed in maths through an emphasis on problem-solving and open-ended investigations. The school has found the primary strategies too pre-scriptive as presented, and that they were tending to stifle teacher creativity. Emphasis on staff-development sessions has been on developing creativity across the curriculum. Often this comes in the form of thinking of creative challenges for children. Recently, Year 5 has tackled the problem of 'How do you measure the speed of sound?' After the investigation Kate wrote that 'when we measured the speed of sound that was basically as creative as you could get'. (An account of how the class tackled the problem appears in the CLEAPPS *Primary Science and Technology* newsletter, Spring 2003.) In science, the school involves local scientists in a Primary Science Day in a local secondary school. A project on 'Ourselves' included Powerpoint presentations by children and a Dance of the Red Blood Cells, jointly presented by Year 5 and Reception children. Real scientists are invited into school to share their experiences with children. Recently, the school has won a Wellcome Foundation Grant for developing their creative science teaching.

Children at Westbury Park are encouraged to think about their own thinking. Here are some views of Year 5 children on what creativity means for them:

■ 'Creative thinking helps me to make connections between things and develop my deepness in thinking.' (Matthew)

■ 'I do not understand why people think only Art and DT are creative because all subjects are creative.' (Rachael)

- Creative thinking is like thinking of all different objects or things in your own way.' (Natasha)

- 'Creativity is stretching further on knowledge, inventing ideas to help your thinking.' (Christopher)

- 'When you think about creative things you also create new brain cells.' (Bianca)

- 'Creativity is the way of thinking out loud original ideas and thoughts.' (Larry)

Many opportunities are given for children at Westbury Park to 'think out loud original ideas and thoughts'. One of the structured ways of doing this is in their philosophy lessons.

Philosophy lessons

Half an hour each week is devoted to philosophical discussion. Stimulus for these discussions can be found in books, such as Robert Fisher's *Stories for Thinking* series, as well as current news stories and topics that children suggest themselves.[1] Philosophy with children links the school's emphasis on values to thinking. It helps promote the speaking and listening skills that underpin success in learning and provides the oral groundwork for effective and imaginative writing. It fosters the discussion skills that underpin citizenship. It engages children in critical and creative thinking about matters of concern to themselves and to others. Marcelo finds that these discussions often spill over into break, lunch and into the home. Children find them, he says, 'deeply motivating'. 'Philosophy is great,' says one of the children, 'it makes us think so deeply and it makes thinking so interesting.'

Recently these philosophy lessons were a feature on the BBC radio programme *Learning Curve*. Teacher Marcelo Staricoff leads philosophical discussions 'about things that really matter' to him and the children. Topics are as varied as the war in Iraq, whether Michael Owen should gamble, whether fish feel pain (so is it right to fish?) or the old conundrum of whether you can step into the same river twice. These are not just lessons in speaking and listening but have also become, for Marcelo, 'more a way of life for us . . . a way of sharing life with the kids and bringing real life into the classroom'.

The children themselves often suggest creative talking points. Georgia says, when asked to think about the value of philosophy, that 'it is really good because you can't be wrong and you can share your opinion and there are no limits to it'. Marcelo finds it helps to bridge the home–school divide. His children often take the philosophical topics and questions home with them to continue the discussion with parents and carers. This is just one way that the school seeks to extend its creative work into the home and the wider community.

Creative learning communities

The school is developing links to a number of other learning communities. It is collaborating with a network of local schools in developing a shared approach to 'Creating the

Learning Curriculum'. They are in a primary/secondary cluster developing policies for the gifted and talented. They have links to the local Scientific Trust in Bristol, to find links to scientists and doctors who could share their work ('A day in the Life of . . .') with classes in school. A local Thinking Skills focus group of teachers and heads has been set up to share ideas about teaching and staff-development activities.

For head Alan Rees, a thinking school is a place that 'focuses on how children learn and develop as lifelong learners'. The various thinking skills initiatives help teachers at Westbury Park School to teach the National Curriculum in more purposeful and creative ways, in stimulating thinking classrooms where both staff and children can be fully engaged in the adventure of learning.[2]

Case Study 2: Ridgeway Primary School

Ridgeway Primary School and Nursery, a large primary school on the outskirts of Croydon, has done just that; since 1998 it has ploughed a lonely furrow in not implementing the literacy or numeracy hours but following its strongly held philosophy that the primary curriculum is made coherent through making creative links between subjects.[3]

Creating the vision

How did they begin this process? As head Anna House explains, 'The best teachers ask questions not only of the children but of themselves'. And among the questions teachers at Ridgeway asked were:

- What sort of curriculum do we want for our school?
- What sort of learners do we want our children to be?
- What does excellent classroom practice look like?

Their answers to these questions became their shared vision. They decided that what they wanted was a creative curriculum that inspired creative learners. One benefit of putting creativity at the heart of the school's approach, says Anna House, is that when teachers are creatively inspired and motivated and can share their practice, it solves the problem of recruitment and retention. Teachers want to work and stay in schools where they feel fulfilled creatively.

Their vision of creativity is not a return to the *laissez-faire* days of the sixties, but a planned curriculum underpinned by a detailed teaching and learning policy 'that was the outcome of a huge amount of professional dialogue'. Teachers work in teams and all are given an afternoon off each week for planning, preparation and assessment (PPA).

'Creativity is a thread running through everything we do,' says Anna House. Another benefit, she says, is that 'it is a way of crediting children with emerging capacities which are often shut down in the school system'. At Ridgeway it is not about having Creativity or Arts Weeks, but about seeking to have 36 creativity weeks each year.

The creative school works through people rather than structures. All are included in the vision – even the school's meals organisers are encouraged to think creatively or, as they put it, 'out of the box'. The creative skills of parents, governors and other visitors are used as creative resources. Teaching assistants (including what they call Advanced Skills Teaching Assistants) are part of the creative team. The idea is to break down stereotypical views of 'learners', 'teachers' and 'assistants'. All in the school are seen as learners, teachers and assistants of each other.

'The more we expect of ourselves and one another the more we can achieve,' reads the lead quote on the school prospectus. How is this vision translated into practice? Elements of what Ofsted described as 'a very high quality curriculum' include:

- Teaching for learning policy;
- Contexts for learning – curriculum planning; and
- Assessment for learning.

Teaching for learning

'Teaching and learning is viewed as preparation for life, not for the next level in a SATs test,' says the head. The focus of the policy is on lifelong learning. As one teacher put it, 'We are about helping children cope with the future'. The school Teaching and Learning policy is detailed (running to 38 pages). It draws on recent research into effective teaching and learning, including theories of multiple and emotional intelligence, learning styles and strategies for effective teaching and for creating a thinking classroom.

The policy stresses equality of opportunity and access to the curriculum, embodying the belief that 'all children are gifted and talented'. They strive to 'take every child as far as they can' rather than focusing on target groups of children. Their focus is on learning not levels. Time allocations are maximised and value is placed on all subject disciplines. Enquiry-based learning provides scope for individual creativity and the development of thinking skills. It assumes that all are gifted and talented in some way and that all have the potential for achievement. Enrichment of the curriculum is provided in lunchtime clubs, which include Japanese (run by a parent), Drama, Chess and Maths. What underlines their philosophy is that children and adults who are stimulated, motivated and challenged, and are given room for creative self-expression, have a healthy self-esteem as well as a continuing thirst for learning.

Creative contexts for learning

In terms of curriculum planning, Anna House explains that 'we make use of guidance – but do not need to be told how to do it'. The aim is to create a holistic curriculum, with themes like spirituality and citizenship linked in all themes. With an agreed framework that reflects an integrated approach using a few sustained themes, short-term planning becomes the focus for teachers' energy and creativity. Sustained themes become important in avoiding the problems of short-term, quickly forgotten, disembedded experiences that are a feature of some approaches to traditional lesson planning (including the Literacy Hour). One teacher observes that 'in writing they have so much to say because they know so much more about it in a sustained theme'.

There are three Contexts for Learning (or sustained themes) each year, making links across the curriculum where possible. The Contexts give coherence to what is learned, and aim to provide a highly planned, broad and balanced curriculum. The Contexts provide the big picture, freeing the teacher to concentrate on the details and day-to-day planning. The Contexts centre on the child's curiosity to find out about the world, and often have a scientific core. Examples of current contexts of study include 'Island destinations' in Year 1, 'Water' in Year 4 and 'Save the Planet' in Year 6. Their medium-term plans start with questions (for example, 'What are the plus, minus and interesting points of living on an island?'), not with learning objectives. They then use the Primary Strategies to inform their planning by highlighting, for example, relevant objectives from the Literacy Strategy. They are not constrained by the suggested yearly progression ('imagined worlds', for example, may be linked to Year 3 rather than Year 4). They are not constrained by the given yearly format. Like the Strategies, their Contexts for Learning are not set in stone. Each year the teaching team review, revise and develop the context themes.

Assessment for learning

Assessment rather than reward systems drives the learning at Ridgeway. Alongside teacher assessment focused on helping children to improve their learning, self-assessment by children is encouraged in all years. Children are encouraged to create their own learning targets. A Year 1 child ends his self-assessment sheet: 'I would like to be a better thinker.' A Year 3 child writes: 'Also I will concentrate harder on the carpet'. Portfolios showing achievements in learning go with each child through the school. These include evidence of creative work across the curriculum. A strong feature of this process is the use of digital photos. Nursery-stage children, as well as teachers, use classroom cameras to record their learning experiences. Photographs are used to record and show evidence of progress. The school uses photos to show parents that learning is a process. In Year 1 children have an impressive display of photos of their sculptures using natural materials inspired by the work of artist Andy Goldsworthy. There is a strong focus, too, on developing visual skills through observational drawing, both to record and to assess visual learning.

There is a focus in the school not only on creative activity, but on the thinking that children need to do to turn experience into learning. For example, on a display of creative work is the heading 'Reception have been *thinking* about . . .'. The language of creativity is used from the early years. One class display is headed: 'I have used careful mark making and shading to *create* the effect of texture in drawings'. Throughout the school there is an emphasis on a thinking visual environment, as one sign says: 'Using your observational skills – what can you see?'. There is much use of pictures for literacy learning, with dialogue and displays accompanied by the question 'What do you think?'

There is a lack of extrinsic reward systems in the school; the focus is on intrinsic motivation. There is an 'open doors' policy in school, in keeping with the spirit of open minds. They believe at Ridgeway that creativity in the classroom is characterised by a focus on:

- *Creative thinking* – encouraging children to behave imaginatively;

- *Cultural learning* – placing a high value on cultural artefacts;

- *Enquiry-based learning* – by the provision of open-ended challenges and problems; and

- *Collaborative learning* – through socially based learning opportunities.

Creativity is underpinned by values of individual choice. From the early years there is a focus on developing independence and self-direction in learning. The school believes in giving both teachers and pupils as much creative autonomy as possible. There are no set playtimes at Key Stage 1, teachers choosing when (and if) to take children out to play according to the needs of the day. In Year 1 children are given their own Inventions Book in which to design creative solutions to problems. The emphasis is on individual creativity. In Year 6 'Shoes' was the context for learning about materials, and for designing a dazzling array of individual shoe creations. There is much evidence here of embodied imagination, that is the physical or kinaesthetic expression of ideas through creating fantasy model environments and constructed designs. From the 'digging patch' in the nursery to Year 6 model shoes there is plenty of scope here for the kinaesthetic learners.

The best advert for the success of a creative curriculum is the response of the children. As pupil Katie wrote (and as quoted at the head of this chapter, and re-stated here) in a recent self-assessment at Ridgeway School: 'I knew the work would be a challenge but I have now learned that I can do anything if I put my mind to it'.

Notes

1 For more on philosophical discussion with children see www.sapere.net www.dialogueworks.co.uk and www.teachingthinking.net.

2 For more on the work of Westbury Park School see Staricoff M. and Rees A. (2003) 'Thinking skills transform our days'. *Teaching Thinking*, Spring, 40–3.

3 *Unlocking Creativity: A report on creative teaching and learning at Ridgeway School*, by Robert Fisher (2003), appeared in *Teaching Thinking*, Autumn, 46–9.

Further reading

Fisher R. (2003) *Teaching Thinking* (2nd edn). London: Continuum.

Jones R. and Wyse D. (2004) *Creativity in the Primary Curriculum*. London: David Fulton.

Learning and Teaching Scotland (2001) *Creativity in Education* (the IDES network).

National Advisory Committee on Creative and Cultural Education (1999) *All Our Futures: Creativity, Culture and Education*. London: DfEE.

Websites

www.artscampaign.org.uk/campaigns/education/pubs.htm

www.artsed.net

www.creativenet.org.uk

www. ides.org.uk

www.ltscotland.com/curriculum/creativity-casestudies.asp

www.ngflscotland.gov.uk/creativity/index.asp

www.qca.org.uk

Appendix: Reviewing creativity

IN REVIEWING PROGRESS IN creativity in schools the Office for Standards in Education (Ofsted) suggest the following questions might provide a basis for discussion and review:

- Does the school have a commitment to promoting creativity: how is this expressed?

- Has creativity been discussed as a concept?

- Have the views of different subject areas been considered?

- To what extent do subject leaders across the curriculum promote creativity?

- Have examples of particularly creative practice been explored?

- How is good practice in creativity to be identified and disseminated?

- What kinds of continuing professional development might be useful?

- What curriculum opportunities are there for subjects to combine meaningfully?

- Is the timetable sufficiently flexible to allow for creative projects to flourish?

- How does the school environment reflect and stimulate the creative work of the school?

- Do pupils have access to suitable accommodation including ICT facilities?

- Have criteria been identified to allow teachers to assess the development of pupils' creativity from year to year?

Source: *Expecting the Unexpected: Developing Creativity in Primary and Secondary Schools*. London: Ofsted

Index

Printed in the United Kingdom
by Lightning Source UK Ltd.
127231UK00007B/45-52/A